LAND YOUR DREAM JOB NOW

Lesley

Best Wishes

Jo.

JO BANKS

LAND YOUR DREAM JOB *NOW!*

Learn the techniques that will put you streets ahead of your competitors…

JO BANKS

First Edition: April 2016

Published by What Next? Media – sales@whatnextconsultancy.co.uk

ISBN: 978-0-9934445-1-7

For Michelle…

Thanks for being there!

"The best way to predict the future is to create it."

(Abraham Lincoln)

CONTENTS

FOREWARD

Welcome to my second book! I only finished and published my first book, *'Thoughts Become Things: Change Your Thoughts, Change Your World'* (available worldwide on Amazon) four months ago, so I'm particularly proud of being able to publish my second book so soon after that.

I'm happy to say that this book was much easier and quicker to write than *'Thoughts'* (which proves that practise does make a difference). My first book took six months, plus the additional time needed for formatting, proofreading, etc. whereas this one virtually plopped out. I wrote 60,000 words in just over a week, which is no small feat ... I literally didn't sleep!

It flowed so smoothly because this book based on the career management programmes that my business, What Next Consultancy (UK) Ltd, has been providing to our clients since its formation in 2009. Although I do have trusted training associates who present many of the workshops, I have personally delivered around 50 and, therefore, decided to write this book based on the information we provide to delegates and during one-to-one sessions. I've also included anecdotes and countless top tips, as well as incorporating feedback from internal recruiters, recruitment consultants, assessors, and HR experts.

HOW AM I QUALIFIED TO WRITE THIS BOOK?

Since setting up What Next, I've personally coached over 1500 people helping them to manage practically every problem you can imagine; a large part of that coaching is focussed on career management. I work with clients to provide them with the tools, techniques and mindset adjustments needed to identify what it is they want and how/where to find and secure it. Whether that entails a sideways move, promotion, or change of career, I help pave the way. I'm also proud to say that I've helped an ever increasing number of clients start their own business.

Before setting up my own business, my background was in senior human resource management (HR), with a career spanning almost 20 years. During that time, I interviewed thousands of candidates ranging from forklift truck drivers to CEOs. Therefore, my extensive experience in recruiting enables me to know instinctively what companies are looking for during the selection process. It allows me to help my clients to maximise their self-promotion, providing them with top tips – often only small things – that will put them ahead of their competitors, enabling them to land their dream job.

OUTPLACEMENT & REDEPLOYMENT

At What Next, outplacement and redeployment programmes form part of our core offering. We provide both off-the-shelf and bespoke career management training to private and public sector organisations, in the course of their ongoing commitment to their employees during change projects and company restructures.

Our programmes include individual workshops on CV writing, interview skills, job hunting, presentation skills, how to start a business, as well as one-to-one career management sessions. We typically provide either redeployment or outplacement programmes, sometimes both. Here's the difference between the two:

- **Redeployment** – Designed to assist employees who are affected by a company restructure and are required to undergo an internal selection process (sometimes referred to as 'applying for your own job'). We will deliver a programme that is tailored to the company's assessment process, providing the essential tools and advice to give employees the best chance of success.

- **Outplacement** – Intended for those employees whose roles have been made redundant. Again, we provide delegates with all the tools, tips, and techniques they need to find and secure the right next role for them.

How we manage these two processes is very similar. We offer three solutions for each:

1. **Full career management workshop programmes** (usually one day). Here's what workshops can be included in each:

Workshop Title	Outplacement Programme	Redeployment Programme
Managing Change	✓	✓
CV Writing	✓	✓
Interview Skills	✓	✓
Job Hunting	✓	✗
Assessment Centre Skills	✗	✓
Starting Your Own Business	✓	✗
Presentation Skills	✓	✓

2. **Workshops plus one-to-one sessions** (face to face where possible) – Delegates usually attend a one day workshop and have follow-up sessions with a dedicated career coach.

3. **One-to-one sessions** – Where only a couple of employees are affected and a full day programme is not viable or where the employees are senior managers, one-to-one sessions are usually preferable.

We also offer each of the individual programme workshops as standalone seminars. For example, organisations that opt for the 'Redeployment Programme' often require a 'Job Hunting' workshop for employees who aren't successful during the internal redeployment process.

ONE-TO-ONE SESSIONS

Depending on the organisation's budget and the client's needs, a dedicated career coach will work closely with individuals on a one-to-one, bespoke basis covering the following areas:

- Assisting clients to 'get clear' about what they want from their next role e.g.:
    - The type of job and content.
    - The kind of company including values and culture.
    - The pay and benefits (remuneration).
- Recognising their transferrable skills.

Producing an outstanding, achievement based CV – which can be written by the coach if preferred.

- Devising a bespoke step-by-step job search project plan.

- Identifying and contacting prospective employers on the client's behalf.
- Advising on bespoke interview preparation.
- Researching the interviewing company, providing the individual with a full report containing vital information.
- Interview feedback review.
- Managing negative emotions e.g. interview nerves, confidence issues, public speaking, and low self-esteem, etc. Helping clients maintain motivation at optimum levels.
- Coaching on personal impact including successful communication/influencing skills, as well as providing guidance on personal presentation.

We offer a comprehensive service, and although we do employ underlying principles, we can tailor our programmes and one-to-one sessions directly to the needs of organisations and individuals. Having that flexibility allows us to deliver effective programmes that achieve sustainable results quickly and simply.

We continually review our processes and content using feedback from our delegates, clients, associates and our extensive contact base within the recruitment industry. These include close links with recruitment consultants, internal recruiters, professional assessors and HR professionals to keep the information we provide current, reflecting the current recruitment landscape.

It's that information and knowledge that I've included in this book. It contains the very best, up to date information available… THIS STUFF WORKS!

THOUGHTS BECOME THINGS

In my first book, *'Thoughts Become Things'*, I primarily focus on how you can change your thought patterns to achieve tangible results, supercharging your performance and elevating your career to the next level. I share the most useful and easy to use tools and techniques from my coaching toolkit to help readers to:

- Recognise and change unhelpful thinking patterns
- Manage stress and anxiety
- Rid themselves of limiting self-beliefs
- Control worrying thoughts
- Gain greater self-confidence
- Silence their inner critic
- Stop self-sabotage
- Be happy NOW!

Having a positive attitude and the ability to think positively about your job search is crucial to achieving great results. Therefore, if you need help addressing any of the issues I've listed above, I recommend that you read *'Thoughts Become Things: Change Your Thoughts, Change Your World'* alongside this book.

As a 'thank you' for purchasing *'Land Your Dream Job Now!'* I have included an edited section from *'Thoughts Become Things'* at the back of this book. This section covers:

- How to change your emotions quickly.
- How to manage negative emotions.
- How to use visualisation techniques.
- Relaxation techniques to help calm your body and mind if you're feeling particularly stressed or anxious.

I chose these topics because they are particularly helpful for keeping you on track during the job hunting process. *'Thoughts Become Things'* is available worldwide from Amazon in paperback or Kindle formats. For more information visit:

www.thoughtsbecomethings.co.uk

FREEBIES

As an additional thank you for purchasing this book, visit **www.yourdreamjob.co.uk** and sign up with a quality email address to receive regular updates and an assortment of useful tools. These include CV template, tracking document, covering letters, etc. delivered straight to your inbox, which are specifically designed to complement this book and help you *'Land Your Dream Job Now!'*

Signing up will add you to our exclusive group of like-minded individuals, who wish to learn the top tips and techniques to enhance their job search and get the edge over their competitors. Head over to the website and sign up now!

www.yourdreamjob.co.uk

INTRODUCTION

"In the end, we only regret the chances we didn't take."

WHY YOU SHOULD USE THIS PROGRAMME

Since the recent recession started back in 2008/2009, the face of recruitment has changed significantly. Recruiters had to rethink their strategies to find low-cost options that would deliver quality candidates. As a result, the recruitment industry had to react quickly in response to the changing needs of its clients.

This change saw a dramatic shift in the way that employers recruited. The use of expensive advertising campaigns and high-cost recruitment consultancies declined almost overnight replaced by more cost-effective attraction methods such as LinkedIn (discussed in detail in Chapter 4) and employee referral schemes.

Many employers initiated a complete halt to all non-critical recruitment, resulting in a candidate-rich environment. As a result, to find and secure the right role, it was necessary for candidates to approach their job search in a new/different way to get the edge over their competition.

Now, thankfully, we are finally seeing economic recovery with companies recruiting non-essential roles again. However, many have taken the decision not to return to their old attraction methods, preferring instead to maintain their existing, low-cost options. Therefore, whether this is your first time in the job market or your first time back in for a few years, this book is for you. It includes practical, simple, down to earth advice that if followed step by step, will give you all the tools you needed to gain a competitive advantage. This information has been proven to work time and time again with literally hundreds of delegates and clients. It is practically foolproof when applied as instructed.

It is relevant to everyone, no matter what level you work at or what job you're looking for - whether you're currently in or out of work, the principles are the same. It will be especially helpful if you know you want a change, but don't know what that looks like or how to go about getting it.

It's intentionally written in simple, uncomplicated terms with a common sense approach that you'll find it easy to follow and implement.

WHAT YOU WILL LEARN

- **Chapter 1 – Managing Change** – This section is particularly useful if you've been made redundant or are currently going through a redeployment process. It clearly explains the emotions you may be experiencing and gives sound advice on how to manage any negative feelings. It also provides practical guidance on how to look after yourself and maintain your motivation.

- **Chapter 2 – Get Clear** – In this section, I help you get clear about the type of job you want, including the role content, the company (including their culture and values) and remuneration. Perhaps more importantly, I will help you identify what you *don't* want. It's common when people first start looking for a new role (especially if they've been made redundant or are unhappy in their current role) to accept the first job offer they receive, only to find that they hate it a couple of weeks or months after starting. This can severely affect their self-esteem and confidence. I help you avoid that scenario with a simple, easy to use exercise designed so that you can quickly identify what you do and don't want from your next role.

- **Chapter 3 - Writing the Perfect CV** – With so much competition from other job seekers, it's no longer acceptable to just regurgitate your job description. Your CV is your primary marketing tool and it's, therefore, important to get it right. In this chapter, I explain how to write an excellent CV; what to include and what *not* to include. Not only will I provide you with an excellent structure, explaining in detail how to complete each section, but I give lots of useful hints and tips which will help your CV stand out from your competitors.

- **Chapter 4 - Managing Social Media** – This is a shorter but important chapter where I describe the do's and don'ts of managing your social media platforms. Prospective employers **will** look at your social media; therefore, presenting the *right*, professional image is essential when you're job hunting.

- **Chapter 5 – Effective Job Search** – As I mentioned previously, the face of recruitment has changed dramatically over the last few years. As a job hunter, you now need to cast your net wider to find the right role for you. In this section, I guide you through how to conduct an effective job search. I have included different job sources, as well as how to manage and plan your time effectively. Good time management will help you avoid potential negative feelings such as overwhelm and panic, allowing you to conduct a quality search rather than it becoming all-consuming. I have also incorporated a critical section on how to get the most out of working with recruitment consultants.

- **Chapter 6 – Assessment Types and Preparation** – As increasing numbers of candidates have entered the job market, with fewer and fewer roles available, recruitment processes have become more sophisticated. To pre-sift applications as cheaply as possible, while ensuring that only the best candidates get through to costly face to face interviews, recruiters now use a far larger range of assessment tools than ever before.

  Proper preparation is vital when it comes to most types of recruitment assessment. For example, did you know that you can prepare of around 80-85% of interview questions? In this section, I'll describe the most typical selection methods, what to expect (how they work) and how to prepare for them to give you the best chance of success.

  I've also included a section on presentation skills which explains a simple six-step process for planning and delivering an effective presentation, including how to answer difficult questions and how to read and manage your audience.

- **Chapter 7 – Interview Skills** – This section is packed full of top tips ranging from what to take into an interview, through to what to wear, how to present yourself and how to communicate effectively, plus how to manage your interview nerves. I also discuss interview feedback and how to incorporate development areas into your future preparation.

- **Chapter 8 - The Job Offer –** Once you get to the job offer stage, you can guarantee that the company is *very* bought into you. It's at this point that you're in the very best position to negotiate the right package. In this chapter, I discuss how to do this effectively. I review employment contracts, references, what to do if a job offer gets retracted or if you change your mind once you've formally accepted.

- **What Next? –** It's imperative that you have a plan that you stick to get the best results from your job search. Here, I supply you with advice on creating a daily activity plan plus how to keep up momentum and motivation; it's not uncommon for job hunters to suffer a slump at some point during their job search.

At the end of this chapter, I've included a list of frequently asked questions that my colleagues and I receive when we're either facilitating workshops or running one-to-one coaching sessions.

- **Additional Resources –** In this section there are copies of all the templates that you will need to manage your job search. These comprise a generic CV template, various tracking documents, power words and template covering letters, etc. You can also get copies of these documents straight to your email inbox when you sign with a valid email address at **www.yourdreamjob.co.uk**.

HOW TO GET THE MOST OUT OF THIS PROGRAMME

The following is a list of my top tips for getting the most out of this programme:

GETTING THE MOST OUT OF THIS PROGRAMME

1. **Do ALL of the steps described** – There may be some things that aren't applicable to you, and it's fine to weed those out. However, this is a complete, comprehensive programme

designed specifically to supply you with the tools and techniques giving you the best chance of success at *'Landing Your Dream Job Now!'* It has been proven to work time and time again when completed in its entirety. If you deliberately miss applicable sections out just because you don't want to do them, it could negatively affect your results.

2. **Job hunting is like anything else:** ***'You get out what you put in'*** - The more effort you put in, the better your results. However, I need to place a caveat here; the effort you put in must be thoughtful and carefully planned rather than using a scattergun, ad hoc approach. 'Scattergun' tends to produce mediocre results at best – job hunting can't be done half- heartedly or without planning.

3. **Take consistent action** - In Chapter 2 - Effective Job Search - I discuss how much time you should spend on your job search each day and how to create an effective plan; *'What gets written down gets done'* (another of my favourite sayings). Having a clear plan and sticking to it will help you keep your search in perspective so that it won't take over your life.

4. **Log your progress** – It's very easy to lose track of jobs you've applied for during a full-on job search. Therefore, it's important to keep a log of:
    - The people you speak to, what you talk to them about

and any follow-up actions required.

- The roles you apply for and when.
- Copies of any applications (CV, application forms and covering letters) that you send.

5. **Stay calm and in control** – For some people, the whole job search process can seem or become overwhelming; that can be because they feel out of control and out of their comfort zone. This book provides you with a firm structure designed not just to help you with the technical aspects of job hunting, but to give back that sense of control.

   I've also included information intended to help you manage your emotions and stay positive throughout the process. In particular, if you start to feel any negative emotions, you might want to visit the section I've included from my first book, *'Thoughts Become Things'* at the back of this book which describes specific exercises to help you gain control over your thoughts and emotions quickly.

6. **Get access to a computer** – Many people now own a laptop or computer at home, however, I'm still surprised by how many people don't. To carry out a successful job search, you must have daily access to a computer and the internet. You'll need a word processing program and have your own email address (see Chapter 4 for more information on email addresses).

If you don't have a computer/laptop, but can afford it, I strongly suggest that you invest in one; even if it's second hand (laptops with basic functions are available as cheaply as £150). If cash is an issue, ask around to see if someone is willing to lend you one for the length of time it takes you to find your next role. Alternatively, most libraries have computers with free internet access. It's essential that you can keep track of your job hunting online and view your emails on a daily basis, or you may miss advertised roles or more importantly, job interview invitations.

TOP TIP

Unless you're under threat of or have been made redundant, I don't recommend using your company computer/laptop to apply for jobs. Many companies monitor email traffic, and I've know employees be dismissed for misuse of company property when they've used company equipment to apply for jobs outside the organisation.

IN SUMMARY

'What Next' has helped numerous people find the right job using the techniques, processes, hints and tips provided in this book. Not everything may work for you as everyone is different. However, I do recommend that you try everything. If it's in here, it's been proven to work consistently.

Don't shy away from activities because you think you may find them a hard to do, or they make you feel uncomfortable. If that's the case, then they're probably the key things where you *should* put your focus. Create a structured plan that you stick to and review it regularly, ticking things off as you do them and keeping copies of any applications. By doing these things, you're much more likely to not only get just any old job but to *'Land Your Dream Job!'*

(N.B. I make no apologies for repeating things that I consider to be important. According to internationally renowned success coach, Anthony Robbins, *"Repetition is the mother of skill."*)

CHAPTER 1 - MANAGING CHANGE

"Whether you think you can or whether you think you can't … you're right!"

FACING REDUNDANCY/JOB LOSS

Facing redundancy or job loss is a massive disruption and hugely upsetting for many people and unfortunately, is a fact of life in our quickly changing world. These days, anyone who has reached the age of 35 and who has not lost their job at least once, is fast becoming the exception.

I was unfortunate enough to be made redundant a few times throughout my HR career (before I set up my own business). Therefore, I have firsthand knowledge of how it feels to be out of work with a mortgage and bills to pay without the luxury of either a redundancy payout, a second income or savings in the bank.

THE KUBLER-ROSS CHANGE CURVE

When we lose a job, we go through different emotional stages. These stages are the same whenever we experience any significant loss. These include the death of a loved one, the loss of a job or income, significant rejection, the end of a relationship or divorce, drug addiction, incarceration, the onset of a disease or chronic illness, an infertility diagnosis and even minor losses.

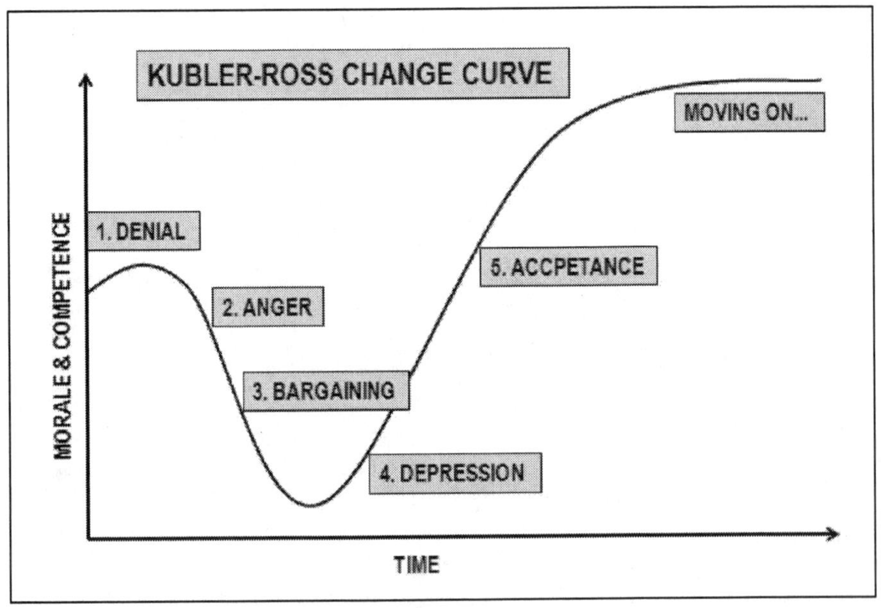

FIGURE 1

Through her studies with terminally ill patients, Swiss psychiatrist Elisabeth Kübler-Ross in her 1969 book, *'On Death and Dying'*, describes the five stages that survivors go through after the death of a loved one (see figure 1 above):

1. Denial

2. Anger
3. Bargaining
4. Depression
5. Acceptance

Kübler-Ross later expanded her model to encompass any form of loss, as she found that the stages were the same no matter the reason.

Regarding job loss/loss of income, people who are affected typically experience the following emotions:

1. **Denial** – *"The Company won't go through with it…"* - This sentiment is quite common when a company makes an announcement about the planned changes, but fails to follow up/communicate quickly concerning the next steps. The longer they leave it (and this is one of the major criticisms I get from employees i.e. the lack of effective communication/information from their employer), the more the affected employees tend to be denial, convincing themselves that it won't happen.

2. **Anger** – *"This is ridiculous; they need me in my role!"* – During this stage, it's not uncommon for some employees to literally 'down tools' and do as little work as possible or to spend most of their working day gossiping and speculating about what's going to happen. I don't advise either of these

behaviours. You may not be aware of it, but if you're going through an internal process, your manager will notice your actions and it could adversely affect your chances of securing a role in the new structure. Also, you should never burn your bridges by acting unprofessionally; you never know who you're going to come across again in the future – it's a small world!

Quite often anger can be coupled with employees deciding to go off sick:

- To 'show the company what they're missing.'
- To make things as difficult as possible for their employer.

Of course, if you are genuinely ill then there's not much you can do about it. However, you'd be amazed how many people take sick leave in protest of the proposed changes. In my experience this usually backfires, as employees who go off sick at such a critical time often report feeling isolated and unsupported, making things much worse in the long run.

3. **Bargaining** – *"If they want me to stay until the end, then I want a bonus."* or *"If they're making me go through an internal process, then I want time off to prepare for interviews."* Companies will often pay a retention bonus to keep key employees until

their leave date – but they don't have to. Others may allow employees go on Garden Leave i.e. stay at home until their contract ends. Note: you can't start any paid work for another company while you're still contractually employed (on Garden Leave) unless you get written permission from your current employer. Often, in this scenario, a company will terminate your employment early, only paying you up to and including the new exit date.

Another point to note is that if your role is being made redundant and you've had confirmation in writing, **the company *has* to give you reasonable time off for job hunting activities** such as interviews, meetings with recruitment consultants, etc.; although they may require evidence of your meetings. A good company will usually allow you time to prepare for any internal redeployment processes.

4. **Depression** – *"This is actually happening, and there's nothing I can do ... I feel so out of control!"* The best way to get through this stage is to plan, using the methods and techniques in this programme. Having a plan and taking consistent action will help you feel more in control. Again, use the techniques in the back of the book to manage your thoughts and emotions.

5. **Acceptance** – *"Well, this is how it is, things aren't so bad."* During this stage, individuals come to terms with what has happened. They have usually found or been placed in another job or established a plan for what they want to do next and are ready to move on.

There is a further stage, 'Moving On' where people have accepted the change and can see that their new setup is better than the old. I can honestly say that I can't think of one person I've worked with who hasn't ended up in a better position mentally, physically and often financially, when they've followed the advice and guidance in this programme. **EVERYTHING HAPPENS FOR A REASON**.

It's important to point out that you can be at any one of the stages at any time i.e. you don't necessarily have to start at denial, and work through each stage consecutively. For example, I was explaining the change curve in a recent workshop, as the delegates were telling each other where they thought they were on the curve; one attendee started laughing (it seemed like he was laughing at his colleagues' misfortune as they were all in anger, bargaining or depression). When I asked him where he thought he was, he replied, *"Acceptance, definitely acceptance!"* When I inquired what the reason was for his assessment, especially given that his colleagues were still at the earlier stages of the curve, he replied, *"I've already got two interviews, so can't understand what's wrong with everyone; I can't see what the big deal is. I know I'm going to be OK!"*

A week or so later, he had his first one-to-one session with me, and he entered the room looking very glum. I asked him what was wrong, especially given that he was so optimistic the previous week. It turned out that he didn't get either of the jobs he had interviewed for and as a result, he slipped from 'acceptance' straight back to 'anger' on the change curve.

Incidentally, I especially like to do this exercise with teams, as it allows colleagues to see why they may be experiencing different emotions at different times, enabling them to support each other more effectively. I also recommend that clients show the change curve to their loved ones. It's often confusing and upsetting to watch those close to us going through a difficult period. Showing them a copy of the curve (Figure 1) can help them understand the emotions and behaviour that you may be displaying and why. I encourage clients to explain that they may be anywhere on the curve from one day to the next (or as one delegate told me, *"From one hour to the next!"*). As a result, they'll be able to see that your feelings and behaviour are entirely natural and to know that it won't last forever; you're simply going through a process.

CHANGE YOUR PERCEPTION

I always get good examples to illustrate the differences in perception when I run career management workshops. I usually start a programme by ascertaining how each person feels about what's happening, and it never ceases to amaze me how the '*situation*' i.e. losing or potentially losing their job, is the same for everyone but how differently each person views it. There are three typical responses:

- ***Delegate 1*** - *"Bring it on! I can finally get to do what I've always wanted to do."* (Excitement/happiness – positive emotions)
- ***Delegate 2*** - *"Oh my goodness, it's the end of the world, I'll never get another job, and then I'll run out of money and then I'll lose my house!"* (Despair/fear – negative emotions)
- ***Delegate 3*** - *"I'm not bothered, something will come up."* (Indifference/resignation – neutral emotions)

The fact remains that the situation is the same for everyone i.e. their role has or is likely to end. It isn't right or wrong, good or bad; it is what it is - it's the *meaning* that they put to it that affects their emotions and their subsequent actions.

I have found, without exception that the people who view their situation in a positive way, always get through the job search process far more quickly than those who see it negatively. Positive people also tend to find exactly the right role with far less effort than those who are negative, as their positivity comes across during their interactions with recruiters.

It's important to point out that how we see the world is a choice. We can *choose* whether view something as a positive or negative; the situation itself is neutral, it's the *meaning* that we put to it that affects how we feel. We aren't born positive/negative or lucky/unlucky; we subconsciously programme ourselves by watching how our parents and primary caregivers reacted to situations as we grew up. If we had negative influences around us, then we are much more likely to view the world in a negative way as an adult.

The good news about this is that if you're a negative person, or you see yourself as being unlucky, it's just bad programming and is totally within your power to change. How do you change from having a negative attitude to a positive one? Well, it's relatively simple (although it takes some practise), you *choose* to!

YOU CREATE YOUR THOUGHTS they don't drop into your head by some mystical force; they are created entirely by you. Therefore, if you have negative recurring thoughts that don't serve you, change them! Wave them away and think of something positive instead. We can't have two thoughts at once, so changing negative thoughts to positive ones as soon as you notice them will help you maintain a more resourceful 'state.' There's more information on how to change your thoughts and manage your 'state' in my book, *'Thoughts Become Things'.*

MANAGING CHANGE

The following is a list of my top tips for managing the change process:

MANAGING CHANGE

1. **Be Positive** – I know it's easy for me to say and if you've just lost your job or are potentially about to lose it, then I can appreciate that you may feel you have nothing to be optimistic about. However, you will come across in a different way to a prospective employer if your overall demeanour is upbeat. Employers like positive people. If you are feeling negative, then that's likely to be what you're projecting which can adversely affect your results, particularly in an interview. Practise pushing those negative thoughts away, replacing them with something positive. The more you do it, the easier it will become.

2. **You get what you think about** – *"Whether you think you can, or whether you think you can't ... you're right."* This statement sums up 'the law of attraction' i.e. think negative thoughts, and you'll

attract negative things, think positive thoughts and you'll attract positive things. It's very simple, and it works without exception.

3. **Visualise a positive result** – If you picture a positive outcome for what you want, your chances of achieving it increase exponentially. We'll talk more about this when we come to interview preparation, as positive visualisation is vital for good interview performance.

   You should start visualising the outcome you want creating a mini video in your mind e.g. see yourself clearly being happy in the job you've always wanted. See it in as much detail as possible – *see what you'd see, hear what you'd hear and feel what you'd feel* if you were in that job. Make pictures big, bright, colourful and clear. Practise seeing them as often as possible throughout the day.

   Create detailed videos of what you might do on a typical day. Again, play them as many times as possible during the day; it will instantly make you feel better, and if done on a consistent basis, will help you feel more optimistic. When you're feeling more confident, it will automatically transfer to your job hunt.

4. **Speak in only positive terms about your job search** – No matter how angry, upset or cynical you may be feeling, people don't want to hear you complaining about it. I'm sorry if that's difficult to read, but they just don't. It makes them feel

uncomfortable, and if you persist, you may find that people start avoiding you altogether.

The more positive you are, the more likely people will want to help you. If you keep complaining, they will want to get away from you as quickly as possible. Even if they don't manage it physically, they'll be thinking it, and if you look closely enough, it will be reflected in their body language. If someone crosses their arms when you're talking to them, it indicates that they're feeling defensive and uncomfortable with what you're saying. If you look at their feet, and they are pointing away from you, that's the direction in which they subconsciously want to go.

5. **Don't be disrespectful toward your current employer** - By all means tell people about your situation but be factual. DO NOT complain about your current employer *especially to a prospective one* (that would mean an instant rejection). It won't show you in a positive light and will negatively affect peoples' opinion of you.

6. **Listen to your gut feeling/intuition** – I get so many clients say that they've applied for a position, but they're not sure if it's right for them. Learn to tune into your gut feeling; it's there for a reason. It's an inbuilt protection tool designed to keep you safe. Therefore, you shouldn't ignore it. The only time I've ever made a wrong decision is when I've ignored my gut

feeling/intuition.

7. **Don't jump into something that isn't right** – Here's one important point to remember that has been proven to be true repeatedly:

    The elation of getting a new job and being able to pay your mortgage/bills only lasts for a maximum of three months. After that, the reality of having to get up every day and do that job becomes reality.

    If you do take the wrong job, the consequences can be profound. One of four things usually happens:

    a. You're likely to be so unhappy that you resign without having another job lined up.
    b. The company won't confirm you in post i.e. you won't complete your probationary period. It's likely that your new employer will know from your non-verbal cues that you aren't happy and will often find some reason not to confirm you in the role.
    c. You'll start looking for another job quickly, which is always difficult to do when you're in full-time employment. There are the practical issues to consider such as the time needed to conduct your job search efficiently, as well as getting time off for an interview, which is likely to be tricky when you've just started a new job.

d. You end up staying in a job you dislike which will ultimately impact negatively not only your work but on your personal life too.

The result of taking the wrong role is likely to adversely affect your self-esteem and confidence (as well as your finances) which can be difficult to recover from. Therefore, if you have the money to be able to hold out a little longer for the right role, then you should *always* do that, without question.

8. **Ignore the 'doom-mongers'** – There are *always* doom-mongers lurking around somewhere, whether at work or your personal life. You know the type of person, they're the ones who say, *"Oh my goodness, I don't know how I'd cope if that were me!" "Oh no this is terrible news, what are you going to do?" "You know there are no jobs out there, don't you? We're in a recession!" "What are you going to do about the children/your mortgage/your bills?"* etc.

The best way to deal with these people is to ignore them. Avoid getting into a conversation with them, do whatever it takes to keep away from them. You have my permission to be a little rude if you have to. If you do find yourself cornered, make an excuse, any excuse and get away from them as quickly as possible.

Doom-mongers are such a common phenomenon that my clients often ask why they behave as they do; after all, it's hardly helping anyone. I think there are two main reasons:

a. They can't help themselves, and they are projecting their worst fears onto you. However, the point to remember is that they are their fears and not yours, and you don't need to hear it or be dragged down by them.
b. Some people just like the drama; it gives them attention (they don't care much about you I'm afraid), they are simply attention-seeking and 'getting in on the act'.

9. **Ignore the current 'recession' obsession** – I get sick and tired of people telling me there are no jobs out there. What a load of rubbish! My company has helped hundreds of people get jobs at all levels and in most professions even at the very height of the recession. We've never failed, not once, so you must completely ignore that fallacy, it's just nonsense. Granted it may take a bit more effort than it might have done a few years ago, but it's eminently possible, especially if you follow this programme and take the actions and advice as described.

TAKE ACTION NOW!

There are lots of things you can do to take control over your situation. Many people struggle because they mistakenly think that there's nothing they can do and therefore, can experience feelings of helplessness. On the contrary, there *are* actions that you can take. Here are my top tips:

TAKING CONTROL

1. **Don't be afraid to ask for help** – We all need help from others from time to time. Don't be afraid to tell people what's happening (however, be mindful that there's a difference between telling people, complaining about it and feeling sorry for yourself). People can't help you if they don't know what's going on and the more people you tell (and I discuss this more in Chapter 5 under 'Networking') the more likely it is that one of those contacts will help you find your next role. I still get clients who think there's a stigma attached to being made redundant; there's no stigma, redundancy is an unfortunate fact of life today.

    If you're feeling particularly stressed, anxious or overwhelmed, don't be afraid to go to the doctor. Mental health problems such as anxiety, stress, and depression are now such common place that they have overtaken back injury as the top reason for working days lost each year due to sickness.

    A doctor will not judge you and will not see it as a weakness but as a genuine illness. We all need a little help from time to time, so if you're struggling, please go and see your doctor. You'll be glad that you did, as there's a good range of help available and it doesn't have to mean medication (although it can be beneficial in the right circumstances).

I have clients referred to me who are finding things difficult. I can usually help them significantly in just one session, by working on their negative thought patterns. You don't have to suffer, it's very common and help is available, but you have to ask!

2. **Tell people/share how you're feeling** – If you do find that you're struggling to come to terms with the change (which is natural), then tell someone; a trusted friend or family member. There's truth in the saying, *'a problem shared is a problem halved'* as talking things through, saying out loud what's bothering you, can really help.

3. **Look after your diet** – When I ask delegates what they can do to help themselves during such a difficult period, at the top of the list is usually either, *"Eat chocolate"* or *"Drink wine"*! While I'm sure these do help some people, I prefer to recommend healthy eating.

   Our diet is one of the first things we let go when we feel stressed or anxious, and we tend to eat junk food and drink more alcohol than usual. However, it is important that you watch your diet during stressful periods. Eating a balanced diet will ensure that you have the right nutrients to provide your mind and body with the fuel it needs to perform well.

4. **Take appropriate exercise** – Again, exercising is another of the first things that can fall by the wayside when we feel stressed. Exercise has been proven to change our biochemistry by releasing endorphins (the feel good hormone) which assist the reduction of cortisol (the stress hormone). The more exercise we do, the better we feel and therefore, the more balanced our thinking will be.

   Exercise doesn't have to mean going to the gym for a gruelling two-hour session. Moving your body e.g. going for a walk for ten minutes, can massively improve your mood. Walking outside, preferably in the countryside, is particularly therapeutic as it connects us to nature and positively affects our mood, changing our biochemistry.

5. **Look after your finances** - Don't put your head in the sand. Sort your finances out as soon as possible, make it a priority. Take a good look at your outgoings and calculate exactly how much you have to spend each month to meet your commitments. Get help from a financial advisor or contact the Citizen's Advice Bureau (CAB) as soon as possible if you think you need financial assistance.

   Money problems never go away, so it's better to sort them out sooner rather than later. If you're concerned about what a financial or CAB advisor may think about you, don't be. They will have heard it all before (and probably much worse), so you shouldn't be concerned. They won't judge you; they're more likely to commend you for taking decisive action and will help design a plan that will work for you and your current circumstances.

6. **Get enough sleep** – When we experience consistent negative emotions, we can find that our sleep patterns are interrupted. It is a common complaint with many people, especially those who are going through significant life changes.

   The majority of my clients who suffer from sleep problems during stressful periods tell me that they don't have a problem falling asleep, but they tend to wake up about 2.00 or 3.00 am, finding it difficult to go back to sleep. When they do finally fall asleep, they usually only get half an hour before their alarm goes off, leaving them feeling dazed and exhausted.

   Before I give you my favourite solution to this problem, it's worth explaining what happens when we sleep (see Figure 2). During non-REM sleep, the body repairs, and re-grows tissues, building bone and muscle and strengthening the immune system. Throughout REM sleep, all of our memories are consolidated, particularly our procedural and spatial memory.

   We tend to spend more time than usual in REM sleep following days when we've been in unusual situations requiring us to learn many new tasks. Although most people don't tend to wake after each cycle of REM, if we're over-stimulated, we may wake up fully, and it could take the length of an entire cycle to get back to sleep. There is an assumption that REM sleep and the dreams we have during REM sleep is physiologically necessary for our healthy brain function.

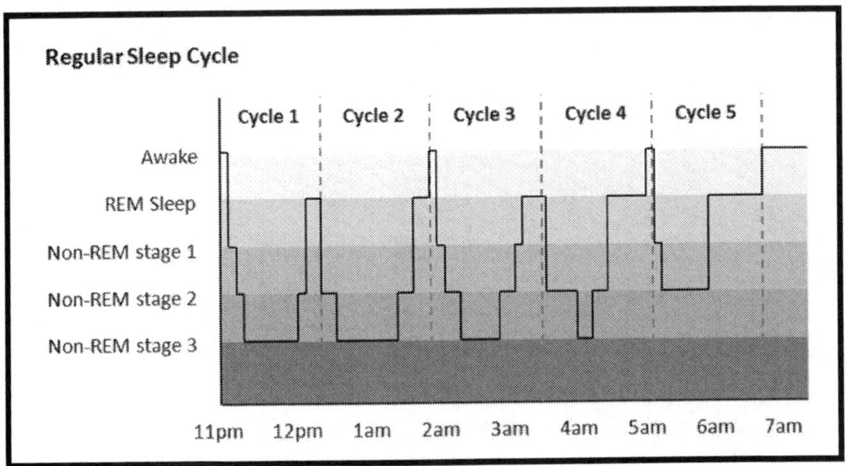

FIGURE 2

When we sleep, the subconscious sorts out all the experiences we've had during the previous day. To use a common metaphor, it files everything away neatly in boxes. Problems occur when your subconscious can't find the right 'box' in which to place an item; that item will usually be something that you haven't been able to resolve during the day.

If you tend to wake at the end of the second sleep cycle (around 2.00/3.00 am) one of the easiest ways to get back to sleep fast, is to leave a notepad by the side of the bed and if you wake up worrying about something, write it down as quickly as possible. Once you've done that, it's usually enough to reassure the subconscious that the item it couldn't 'file' has been dealt with, allowing you to go straight back to sleep.

Don't wait too long to write it down after you wake and stimulate yourself too much by getting out of bed or turning on the TV. If you do this, it may mean that you have to wait until the next sleep cycle before you fall asleep again (typically 1.5-2 hours). Whenever I teach this simple technique to clients, most tell me that they only needed to do it for a couple of nights, and the problem resolves itself.

There's a more in-depth section regarding sleep in my book, *'Thoughts Become Things'*.

CHAPTER 2 – GET CLEAR

"Don't pick a job with great vacation time; pick one that doesn't need escaping from."

One of the most important things to do before you even begin your job search is to get entirely clear about what it is that you want from your next job. Maybe even more importantly, get clear about what you *don't* want.

When you're completely sure, you won't be tempted to take something just because it's '*a job*'. If you take just anything, there's a real chance that you'll start the new job only to find that you're terribly unhappy a couple of months in, bitterly regretting your decision.

Often, a client will come to me because they think they don't know what to do next; however, are frequently very clear about what they *don't* want. Writing down what you don't want can be a great place to start if you're struggling to decide what to do next.

I use the following simple exercise to help my clients get clear about what they want from their next role. When you complete this activity, it will give you clarity around what's important to you and once you know that, it's much easier to find/attract the right role for you.

GET CLEAR

Take three sheets of A4 paper and write one of the following headings on each sheet:

1. Job Content
2. The Company
3. Remuneration

Next, draw a line down the centre of each sheet creating two columns on each page. At the top of the first column write, ***'What I want'*** and at the head of the second column write, ***'What I don't want'***.

1. **Job Content**

   In this section, you will list the types of things that you want to do in your job role i.e. the tasks/activities/responsibilities. You'll include things like:

- The 'level' or seniority of the position e.g. team leader/ manager/executive etc.
- The key tasks that you would want/would not want to do. For example, presentations, administration, project work, telesales, business development, day to day operations, face to face sales, national/international travel, report writing, project management, full time/part time, days you want to work, contract, interim, permanent, temporary, etc.
- The key responsibilities e.g. managing a team, budgetary control, strategic planning, etc.

It's of equal if not more importance, to note down the things that you *don't* want from your next role in the *'What I don't Want'* column.

Next, star (*) the most important items on each side. These should be the things that you really *must* or *must not* have as part of your new role. Some things will always be negotiable; others won't. Therefore, you should only star something if you consider it to be vital. For example, if it's important not to be away for more than two nights a week, and you find a role that means being away for four, then you should automatically disregard that position. When you are clear about what you absolutely must/must not have from your next role; you will be able to be more selective, potentially avoiding making the wrong decision.

JOB CONTENT (The 'tasks' you will be carrying out, including day to day activities/responsibilities.)			
What I want…	*	**What I DON'T want…**	*
Project work	*	*Day to day operations*	
National travel		*To be away from home for more than two nights a week*	*
Budgetary control	*	*Not having budgetary control*	*
Manage a team		*International travel*	

'Job Content' is likely to be the longest of the three lists. You should keep it in view during your job search, adding to it as you make additional distinctions. You should be able to list at least three-quarters of an A4 page under ***'What I want'***.

2. **The Company**

Here you should list the 'values' that you want in your new employer. We rarely leave our current jobs because we don't like the role (unless we were made redundant), but because our values no longer align with our employer's. Without being clear on the values that are important to you, you could end up in the right role, but in the wrong company. Values for the purpose of this exercise include:

- **The culture**
  - Learning and development (further training and investment in you)
  - Social reasonability
  - Diverse workforce
  - People-centric/valuing employees
  - Supportive
  - Work/life balance

- **The people**
  - The type of individuals you want to work with
  - Type/size of team
  - Type of manager you want

- **Hygiene factors**
  - The location/ how far you're willing to travel to get to work.
  - Expense policy (don't overlook the importance of this one!).
  - The environment (e.g. own office, shared office, factory, shop size, etc.).

This list is not exhaustive. Add the things that are important to you and, of course, list what you absolutely can't live with on the other side of the page. A good example to illustrate this is a client who had been working in the 'City' (London's financial district), and he knew that he couldn't work in that environment again. He wanted a company that valued its employees and where he felt part of a team, rather than feeling the need to be in constant, unhealthy competition with his colleagues. Therefore, starred the *'Work in the City' on his* ***'Don't Want'*** *list.*

3. **Remuneration**

Remuneration encompasses the salary and the benefits that go with the role. Again, you need to note what's important for you. It might be Private Health Care, a particular make of car, car allowance, pension, the number of holidays, etc.

One critical thing to point out here is: **DON'T DROP YOUR SALARY INITIALLY**. You should use the opportunity to increase your salary, not drop it. Applying for a new role outside your current company is one of the best times to bump yourself up the ladder. I don't mean you should apply for positions that pay £10K+ more than what you currently earn. Unless you significantly underpaid in your current position and are confident that you will be able to deliver in a significantly bigger role. However, you may wish to consider applying for jobs with salaries up to £5K more than you currently earn. It's likely that you will be able to perform the tasks within that role comfortably, and it would be a realistic increase.

So many clients, especially those in redundancy situations say to me, *"I want £x salary, but I'd be happy to drop to £x because I've looked at my finances and think I can manage it."* Why on earth would you consider cutting your salary before you've even started your job search? That should always be a last resort unless you have a valid reason, e.g. you wish to reduce your hours or take a job with less responsibility in order to achieve a better work/life balance.

Most people find that they don't have much to write in the ***'Don't want'*** column in this section, but they will 'star' a few of their must haves. The remuneration list is usually the shortest of the three. Here are some examples of what you may want to write here:

- Salary £x
- Bonus
- Private Medical Insurance
- Private Health Care
- Car
- Car allowance
- Pension
- Shares
- Number of holidays
- Sick pay
- Maternity benefits
- Supported learning

For some clients (the ones who live for their holidays) the number of holidays is a deal breaker for them, too few and they won't even apply for the role. In those circumstances, they would 'star' holidays in the want column and list the desired amount. For others, may be continued development e.g. funding to complete a qualification.

An example 'Get Clear' form is available in the 'Additional Resources' section of at the back of this book. Alternatively, you can receive a copy sent directly to your inbox, along with other useful documents referenced throughout the book, when you sign up to receive regular 'Dream Job' updates at **www.yourdreamjob.co.uk**

IN SUMMARY

Once you've thoroughly completed this exercise each time you apply for a role, check to see if the key aspects fit with what you've listed. If it contains too many items from your *'don't want'* list, especially the ones you 'starred', ignore it and move on to the next. Getting clear is a critical first step to landing your dream job.

CHAPTER 3 – WRITING THE PERFECT CV

"If opportunity doesn't knock, build a door."

The majority of people I work with have never had any formal CV training, and if they have, it was before the latest recession. In fact, many don't even have a CV because they've been in the same role/company for many years. If they do, it's often significantly out of date, and they don't know where to start updating it so end up just adding additional roles to an already overly long CV.

Occasionally a client will tell me that employees have opted out of attending a CV workshop because they have 'a friend' in HR or a management colleague who has looked over their CV and they think they don't need any help. They don't need it, of course, until they get the feedback from their co-workers about what I cover!

Many managers including HR professionals can be terribly out of date when it comes to the requirements of a CV in today's competitive recruitment market. Therefore, I'd be very careful if you're thinking about skipping this section because you already have a CV, or someone's checked it for you and they think it's great.

It's no longer enough or acceptable to just uplift your job description and insert it into your CV, which is unfortunately what most people still do. That's just sloppy and lazy and will not give you a competitive advantage. CV's these days have to be **ACHIEVEMENT FOCUSED.**

WHY CV'S GET REJECTED

Companies discard CVs for many reasons including:

1. **They are too long or too boring** – Your CV should be no longer than two sides of A4 paper (two and a half at the very most if you have numerous qualifications). I often hear cries of horror when I talk about this in CV workshops. People think that they can't reduce their whole career into two pages. However, if a 55-year-old CEO of a large multi-national corporation can, you can! You have to be selective about what you write, only including relevant information that corresponds to the requirements for the role(s) you are applying for.

TOP TIP

2. **They aren't tailored to the position/contain irrelevant information** – *This is the overriding reason why CVs are rejected.* If you include information that isn't relevant to the position you're applying for, you're completely wasting valuable space. Your CV is a marketing tool and should be used to provide as much evidence as possible (skills, experience, qualifications) proving to the recruiter why you are suitable for that particular role. Therefore, if it contains irrelevant information, it's not likely to get you past the pre-sift stage. The recruiter won't be able to see how your skills and experience match their criteria. You can't list everything you've ever done; you simply don't have the room. Therefore, it's of the utmost importance that you only include information that's relevant to the role for which you're applying.

Many clients struggle with this one; they want to include everything, even if it's not relevant because they think it looks impressive. On the contrary, if a recruiter can't see immediately (on the first page) how you match their essential requirements it's likely that your application will be rejected. Any additional information i.e. anything that's not essential to the role should be saved for discussion at the interview.

If there is more than one type of position that you could apply for, each requiring slightly different skills/experience, there are two options:

a. Write one, extended CV, containing all your skills, experience, and qualifications (this could end up being four pages long). Each time you apply for a new role, edit the CV down to two pages reflecting the skills/experience required for that position.
b. Create more than one CV tailored to different roles e.g. I recently worked with a client who had general management and project management knowledge. He didn't mind which role he ended up with, so we did two CVs containing specific skills and experience matching each of those job titles.

Here's an excellent example to illustrate the importance of tailoring your CV. One of my clients was being made redundant from his role of 'mailroom manager' within a large corporation. When we had our first one-to-one meeting, he told me that he'd been applying for supermarket management roles, as he'd done that for some years before moving to his present job. He was upset because he had applied for forty vacancies. However, he hadn't had one interview, and couldn't understand why because he had the skills and experience, albeit a few years earlier.

When I looked at his CV (it was five pages long) it wasn't until the third page that I found his supermarket management experience. It was easy to see why he'd been passed over for an interview; it wasn't immediately apparent where his skills and experience matched those required for the roles he was applying for.

We re-wrote his CV putting his relevant experience on the first page, and he started applying for more supermarket management vacancies immediately. Within three days he had two interviews and was offered both jobs within a week. That's the power of a 'tailored' CV.

TOP TIP

Recruiters will not search to see how you fit their criteria; you have to put it right on the first page so that they can see it immediately.

3. **They are poorly presented/have a poor layout (typos/font/ paper/print, etc.)** – When I tell clients that their CV must be no longer than two pages, occasionally I'll get presented

with two pages of tiny type font, with the margins pushed out to the edge of the page. That's not acceptable. CV's should be easy to read, with good spacing, using the right type font and size. Use typeface Arial pt 10 or 11 or Calibri pt 11 (do not use Times Roman, its old fashioned and will make you look outdated), with NO typos, spelling mistakes or errors of any kind.

It's tough to see our own mistakes, so you should get someone who has a good command of written English to read it, checking for errors including spelling and grammar. Issuing a CV full of spelling and grammatical errors is unacceptable, it will be rejected no matter how good your skills and experience may be.

If you're printing your CV (you should always take at least two printed copies to interviews), make sure you use a heavier weight, good quality paper, don't just use cheap flimsy photocopy paper. Good quality paper will tell the interviewer that you are professional and pay attention to detail. Also, make sure that copies are in pristine condition with no folds and no ragged edges – staples or paper clips are fine. The presentation is paramount.

4. **They arrive too late** – Don't think that you can just sneak an application in after the closing date. The deadline is there

for a reason, and if you fail to meet it, it tells the prospective employer that you can't meet deadlines – it's as simple as that.

USING POWER WORDS

You can use power words to supercharge your applications. As you only have a limited amount of space on a CV, frequently you can replace three or four smaller words with one excellent power word.

Following are some examples of power words; a more comprehensive list is available in the 'Additional Resources' section of this book or sign up at **www.yourdreamjob.co.uk** to receive a copy straight to your inbox.

- Delivered
- Implemented
- Administered
- Structured
- Budgeted
- Analysed
- Completed
- Built
- Transformed
- Conducted
- Managed

Keep a copy of the full list with you while you're writing your CV, covering letters and applications as it will help you to eliminate repetitiveness. Using power words expands your vocabulary making your written documentation look more professional than it may otherwise be.

Occasionally, I do get clients who say, *"But my CV doesn't sound like me! Shouldn't my personality come through a bit more?"* In short, no! **The sole purpose of a CV is to get you an interview.** It's a marketing tool, and you should use it as such. A well written, factual, well laid out CV, tailored to the role you're applying for is exactly what your CV should be.

WRITE IN THE THIRD PERSON

Before I start to talk about the CV structure, there is one important thing that I must cover:

YOUR CV MUST BE WRITTEN IN THE THIRD PERSON

What that means is that you must not include 'I,' 'me,' 'my,' 'me,' 'we,' 'my,' etc. and must not mention your name other than at the top of the CV, above your contact details. Writing in the *first* person will make your CV look out-dated and very unprofessional. This rule also goes for your 'Summary Statement' – for some reason, many people will write the majority of their CV in the third person and then convert to the first for their 'Summary Statement' – that's wrong.

I usually get gasps of horror when I tell clients that they can't use 'I,' 'me,' 'my' and some struggle transferring their CV to from first to the third person. However, I have an easy solution; when you take the 'I,' 'me,' 'my' out of a sentence it usually still makes complete sense. For example, if you have a sentence that says, *'I designed a new process'* just remove the 'I' to read, *'Designed a new process.'*

When you've finished your CV, give it to someone else to read and tell them about the 'I,' 'me,' 'my' rule. Ask ask them to pick out any that you may have left in (I'll guarantee that there'll be at least one that you've missed if you wrote the original in the first person).

THE CV STRUCTURE

There is no right or wrong when it comes to CV structure; there are many different suggested layouts available. However, I know without a doubt that the one I share here has been proven to work and help people to get an interview literally thousands of times.

I recommend five different sections:

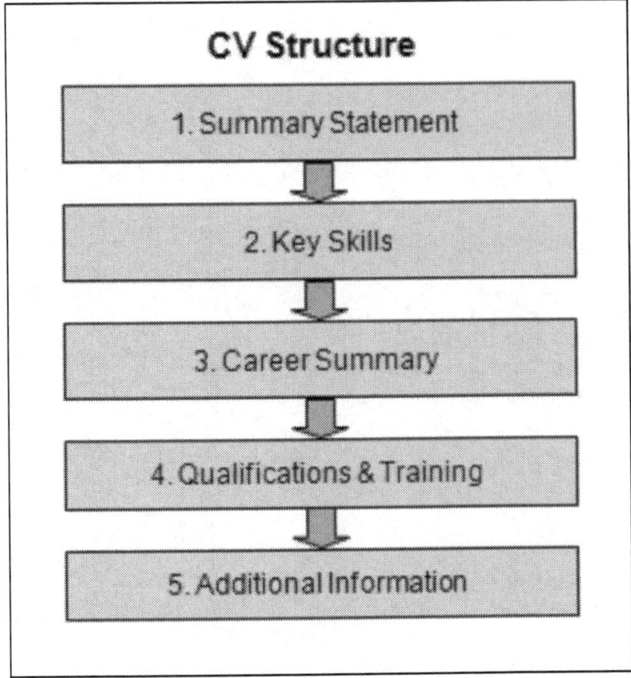

FIGURE 3

I realise that writing a CV when you haven't done one in a long time or if it's your first, can be a bit daunting; therefore, I've broken each section down, providing you with clear guidelines as to what to contain in each.

SECTION 1 - SUMMARY STATEMENT

The 'Summary Statement' is the first thing that the recruiter reads and, therefore, it must clearly explain who you are and why you are suitable for the role. **This section absolutely must be tailored to the position.**

In essence, the summary statement should consist of one paragraph, containing three points:

1. **What are you?** - Your job title or something that reflects a generic title for the type of work you do. There can often be different job titles for the same role depending on the company. For example, in one company an HR Business Partner may be the same as a Head of HR in another, which may be the same as a Senior HR Manager somewhere else. In these circumstances, I'd use a more generic title of 'Senior HR Professional'.

   Another example of using a nonspecific job title is if you are seeking a general management position that requires standard management skills. In this case, I would write 'experienced manager' rather than writing a particular job title that may be only applicable to your company. You don't want to pigeon-hole yourself if there is more than one type of role you may be suited to.

   However, if your job title *is* the same as the positions you are applying for e.g. personal assistant, architect, accountant, general manager, you would naturally write that. (I'll talk more about job titles in Chapter 5 – Job Search)

2. **What's different about you?** – Here you should write what makes you different from your competitors. That could be

your skills, time in the role, particular projects delivered, the size of the team or budget that you manage, anything that demonstrates your skills and the size of your job.

3. **What's next for you**? – The type of role/company/culture you are looking for next. This last bit is optional, and some clients choose not to include it in favour of adding more information to No 2 above.

TOP TIP

DO NOT include things that the recruiter could perceive as subjective. Whatever you put must be factual and be backed up later in the CV. Examples of what **NOT** to write are:

- Hardworking
- Trustworthy
- Dedicated
- Outgoing
- Conscientious etc.

Including these types of words is nonsense as they are just your point of view, and for all the recruiter knows, you could have completely made them up! Whatever you write should be factual and be backed up later in your CV.

I have to mention my personal pet-peeve here; please don't put *'Works well alone or as part of a team.'* Of course, you do! Who doesn't? Oh my goodness, I hate that term and so do many recruiters. It's a complete waste of space on a CV and something that most people (for some reason) *think* they should include. It says nothing about you and is something that's just regurgitated rubbish which turns recruiters off. They are looking for originality, and you need to stand out not be the same as every other applicant. I would estimate that at least nine out of ten people have that statement somewhere on their CV. Remember you only have limited space, so you need to use it wisely, including facts that can be backed up, not including statements that say nothing about you, your skills and experience.

Here is a couple of examples of what you might put in your 'Summary Statement':

Example Statement 1:

"**(1)** *A qualified Prince2 Project Manager* **(2)** *with 15 years experience in a variety of industries including logistics and manufacturing. With a proven track record of leading high performing multifunctional teams and managing continuous improvement.* **(3)** *Looking for the opportunity to utilise skills in a complex, multi-faceted change environment."*

Example Statement 2:

"**(1)** *An experienced Administrator* **(2)** *with an extensive background in building customer relationships, managing third party contractors and* *working within budgetary constraints. Possesses exceptional communication and organisational skills gained while working in a pressurised, customer focused environment.* **(3)** *Looking for the opportunity to develop existing skills and experience within a challenging environment."*

Obviously, you won't put the (1), (2), and (3) in yours I've just done that to demonstrate the three different parts i.e.:

1. What you are
2. What's different about you
3. What's next for you

TOP TIP

Although this section is the first thing on your CV after your name and contact details, it's often easier to write *after* you've completed the other parts. Therefore, you might want to write the next parts and then come back to it. Make sure that you do come back to it, though – don't leave it out as it's vital.

SECTION 2 - KEY SKILLS

The 'Key Skills' section is another part that you *must* tailor to the role. The easiest way to do this is to look at the 'essential' skills in the job advertisement, person specification or job description and list them in bullet point form (as long as you have those skills). You will demonstrate them later in the 'Career History' section.

Writing the key skills that the recruiter is asking for is a little psychological trick that should get you through the initial pre-sift of applications. If you list your skills towards the top of your CV, it immediately tells the recruiter that you have what they're looking for, saving them valuable time and energy searching through your CV. They can see that you have the skills they're looking for right up front.

Often, in larger companies the pre-sift process is done via a computer program. The recruiter feeds a list of keywords into the program if the program finds enough of those words in your CV; it will automatically go through to the next stage.

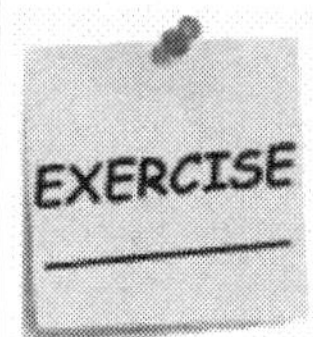

KEY SKILLS

In the absence of a job description/person specification, make a list of your eight top skills and record them in bullet form. To help you do this, I've made a note of the most requested key skills collated from reviewing one hundred typical job descriptions used by one of our large corporate clients:

Administration	Communication	Problem Solving
Prioritisation	Analytical	Networking
Project Management	People Management	Compliance
Customer Service	Risk Assessment	Risk Management
Managing Deadlines	Diary Management*	Strategy/Vision
Report Writing	Change Management	Leadership
Budget Management	Systems Knowledge	Product knowledge
Influencing & Negotiation	Financial Management	Performance Management
Relationship Management	Stakeholder Management**	Planning & Organisation

*Diary management means managing a diary for one or more people other yourself e.g. a PA or secretary would list 'diary management' as a key skill.
** Stakeholder management is where you manage different key contacts typically both internal and external to your business. Don't get this confused with networking which is something completely different.

This list is not exhaustive, and you can add your own. If you have a profession, it's very likely that you'll have additional, specific skills related to your job. My list is for guidance only, designed with the intention of getting you started.

On your CV, you should list the bullets side by side in two columns. As you only have limited space you can't afford to waste it by putting each skill on a new line. The easiest way to do this is to create a table, make your list then remove the table's lines. Using some of my skills, this is how I would lay it out on the page:

• Coaching	• Strategic Planning
• People Management	• Training Design
• Influencing & Negotiation	• Business Development
• Writing	• Public Speaking

Once I've created the table, I would then remove the lines so that on my CV, it would appear like this:

KEY SKILLS

- Coaching
- People Management
- Influencing & Negotiation
- Writing
- Strategic Planning
- Training Design
- Business Development
- Public Speaking

WRITING YOUR 'KEY SKILLS'

1. 'Key Skills' is a part of your CV that you **must** tailor to the role you are applying for.

2. It's likely that you will have far more than eight essential skills, and you may wish to write more when you're first creating your

CV. You can then take out any that aren't applicable when you're applying for a particular role.

3. If you have a job description/person specification or job advertisement, match your skills to the 'essential' skills that the recruiter stipulates (provided that you have them).
4. List your key skills in a table format on your CV so that you have two per line. That way you aren't wasting valuable space.

SECTION 3 - CAREER SUMMARY

This part of your CV demonstrates your job history, including your current and previous roles and is where you get to illustrate your skills and achievements. It's this section that shows the recruiter what they are 'buying' if they select you.

TOP TIP

This section must be achievement focused i.e. **don't just write your job description, you must list your biggest accomplishments**.

I make no apologies for repeating myself here; gone are the days when you could just copy and paste your job description. That's no longer acceptable and isn't likely to get you through a tough selection process. Recruiters now want to see your

ACHIEVEMENTS, what you have done in your current and previous roles that have added value. If you write your accomplishments rather than your duties, it will undoubtedly put you ahead of the competition (unless they've read this book too!).

STRUCTURE FOR YOUR CURRENT AND PREVIOUS ROLE

Always start with your most recent/current job first and then work backwards. For your current and previous role (if you've been in your current position less than ten years) use the following structure (I will discuss older roles later in this section):

1. **Brief summary of the role showing size and scope**

    - You may wish to include one line about your current company. Providing this information is of particular importance to management, senior management and professional roles as it gives the recruiter and idea of the size of the organisation. Include facts such as the number of employees and locations, turnover, etc.

    - Explain what you're responsible for/your *key* duties. Don't list everything you do. This section should just be a *summary* and contain the most important aspects/duties/responsibilities of your role. For example, if you manage people, you don't need to list all the tasks involved such as timesheets, holidays, disciplinaries, grievances, performance management, etc., you simply need to write 'managing a team of X' or 'people management' as everyone knows what managing a team involves.

- If 'administration' is part of your role, you don't need to write, photocopying, filing, typing reports, etc., again everyone knows what tasks it entails, just write 'administrative duties.'

- Include as many facts and figures as you can (especially for management/professional/executive roles), e.g. the number of people you manage, the size of your budget, the number of locations in your remit, your portfolio size, etc. This information shows the employer the size of your role.

- TOP TIP This part should be no longer than one paragraph. It can be quite tight to get everything you need to in such a short space, and some clients can struggle with this. That is until I ask the question, *"What would you tell me that you do if I met you in the street? How would you explain the key responsibilities/duties of your job to someone who doesn't know you?"*

I appreciate that this can be difficult if, in the past, you transcribed the key tasks from your job description. Therefore, it may be helpful to think what you say to people when they ask you what job you do. You may need to add a little more detail e.g. essential duties, the size of the role, etc., but in essence, you won't go wrong if you follow this advice.

You may want to look at your current job description and see if the role summary or role purpose fits here. But, please **don't** start writing bullet points containing your responsibilities. That isn't what I'm suggesting, that's the old-fashioned format that many people still insist on using.

2. **Your achievements –** This part is the most vital part of your CV as it's your chance to impress prospective employers. This section should include:

   - **Eight bullets demonstrating your significant accomplishments** – What I mean by this are the things that you have delivered in your role that have added value. Thinking about your achievements could be a new concept for you as you may not even realise that you have any. However, everybody does, no matter what their job, otherwise there would be no point in a company having your role within their structure.

Many clients find it difficult to think about what they've achieved. When I start to coax it out of them, they'll often say, *"But that's just my job!"* Yes, it may be, but just because something is part of your duties doesn't mean that you haven't achieved it.

There are some actions you can take to help remind yourself of what you've accomplished in your present role:

- **Ask your Manager** – He/she should be able to tell you/remind you.
- **Ask your colleagues** – It's likely that they've either been part of any activities with you or you've told them about what you've been involved in.
- **Review your performance management/job appraisals** - Most large companies have a formal appraisal process and therefore, your achievements should be contained in the documentation. If you don't have a copy of the paperwork, you can usually request it from your manager or HR department.
- **Look back through your diary** - What meetings have you attended in the last couple of years? Quite often

as soon as we finished a project or a piece of work, we completely forget about it and quickly become engrossed in the next. Looking back through your diary is a great way of reminding yourself what you've been involved in and your achievements.

- **Each bullet should show a business benefit** – If you don't have a management role, then you may find this a little tricky as often we don't ask *why* we are required to do something, we just do it! If you're unsure, ask your manager (if possible) or your colleagues.

- **Demonstrate different aspects of your role/your key skills** – This is where you get the opportunity to demonstrate the key skills that you mentioned in the second section. Each bullet should evidence a different skill if possible.

TOP TIP

- **Explain each achievement in no more than two sentences** (these are bullet points, not paragraphs). The bullet point should contain two parts:

    - **What you did** – Succinctly explain what you did. Use your power words here, starting bullet points with verbs like Delivered, Negotiated, Designed, Implemented, Conducted, Completed, etc.

  - **What the outcome was** – Include the business benefit i.e. what the business gained by your achievement. Add as many facts and figures as you can here if you don't know them or can't remember, go and find out! Numbers are always an eye catcher. You should include percentages, cost savings £X, examples of where you've met/exceeded budget and by how much, and the results of critical negotiations, KPI achievement (Key Performance Indicators) and targets met/exceeded.

- **Meet the 'So What?' test** – If you can say, *"So what?"* after reading each bullet, then you haven't put enough information. You need to drill down and think about why you did what you did and what the outcome/ benefit was to the business. I drive my clients mad with this one; I'll keep asking, *"So what?"* until we've established the absolute business benefit.

Here are some example achievements taken from actual client CVs:

- Successfully established and grew a design, manufacturing and retail company from an original partnership to an organisation employing a workforce of over forty people. Achieved year on year increase in turnover from £500,000-£750,000 within twelve months.

- Introduced a new appraisal process. Increasing employee completion from 38% to 92% within twelve months and enabling structured succession planning.
- Executive lead for a major change programme incorporating the restructuring of teams and directorates, managing redundancies and recruitment processes. Delivered a structure which is fit for purpose enabling £1 million costs savings within three months.
- Delivered a new business improvement project over a six month period. Allowing increased capacity and cost savings in excess of £200k.
- Managed a large scale IT recruitment project (60 specialist roles). Delivered on time and within budget.
- Planned and implemented £100k upgrades to communal heating systems. Ensured the most efficient option for each scheme, with no disruption to customers.
- Reviewed and redesigned the company's filing system, resulting greater efficiency and substantial time savings.

- Successfully negotiated with suppliers regarding their pricing structures to reduce costs resulting in greater efficiency. Delivered cost savings of 5% on the previous year.
- Worked diligently, to continually meet and exceed KPIs of eighty picks per hour.
- Successfully managed the yearly 'Company Fun Day' which contributed to the achievement of the company's social charter.

PREVIOUS ROLES UNDER TEN YEARS OLD

For the role before your current or last one (if you're currently out of work), you should follow the same structure as described above but with fewer achievements i.e. **the brief summary of the role showing size and scope, together with four to six key achievements.**

If the next previous position (three roles ago) is less than ten years old and is similar to the roles you are applying for now, then write the key responsibilities/purpose, but only include two-three achievements.

The nearer your previous positions are to being ten years old, the fewer achievements you need to add. That is unless one of those jobs is the same or similar to the type of role you want to apply for now, but which is different to what you have been doing for the last few years (see my 'mailroom manager' example earlier). If that's the case, then you need to include six-eight achievements.

If you have had more than three roles in the last ten years, for those older jobs, you only need to write the 'key responsibilities' section and leave out the achievements.

HOW TO WRITE OLDER ROLES

For jobs that are more than ten years old, it may not be appropriate to write as much information, especially if those roles have nothing to do with the types of positions you are applying for now. Therefore, just write the **brief summary of the position showing size and scope** as mentioned above. Again, unless vacancies you're applying for now, are similar to a previous position (again think about the 'mailroom manager' example), you don't need to include any achievements.

For roles that are over 15 years old, you may wish to only write the dates, the company, and your job title, as it's not likely that they have any bearing on the roles that you are applying for now.

For example:

Job Title Company, Location	**Date**
Job Title Company, Location	**Date**

Put the dates of your positions on the right hand-side. The reason for that is two-fold:

1. Sometimes recruiters can get hung up on how long you've been in a role. Putting dates on the right-hand side makes them stand out less, as we read left to right. This advice is particularly useful if you've been in the same company for a long time as some prospective employers may think that you've been 'institutionalised' and, as a result, will find it difficult to adjust to a new company or only know one way of doing things. Alternatively, if you've had a few jobs in a short space of time, it could be considered that you have no 'staying power' and are likely to leave.
2. It gives you a few lines back! Remember space is short with only two sides of A4 available. Therefore, you can't afford to waste whole lines on writing dates.

N.B. Always check that your dates are correct. Writing incorrect dates is a common error that many applicants make.

HOW FAR SHOULD YOU GO BACK WITH YOUR WORK HISTORY?

How far you go back on your CV is entirely up to you. The Equality Act 2010 makes it unlawful to discriminate against employees, job seekers, and trainees because of age, e.g. rejecting an applicant because they are 'younger' or 'older' than a relevant and comparable, existing employee. However, if you're older and have been working for 20/30 years or more, you may not want to highlight that fact to a prospective employer.

If this is the case for you, consider excluding jobs that you had in the first few years after leaving school/higher education as it's likely that those roles don't relate to what you're doing now. For example, before I started my career in HR, I was a Personal Assistant to a Director of a large company. As my career in HR progressed, my previous PA role became irrelevant, and therefore, I remove it from my CV.

I know I keep saying it, but you only have two pages to provide as much *relevant* information as possible, information that will help you to get the job you are applying for *now*. N.B. some organisations including banks, police, fire, HM forces may require your complete career history.

SECTION 4 - QUALIFICATIONS & TRAINING

In this section you are going to list:

- Formal qualifications e.g. degree(s), GCSEs, O Levels, A Levels, CSEs, etc.
- Formal career based qualifications e.g. CIPD, ATT, CIMA, NEBOSH.
- Work based training (in-house courses) **undertaken less than five years ago** - anything older than five years will not be relevant. For example, I once had a client who included an employment law seminar he attended six years ago – employment law changes every six months and therefore, it was entirely out-of-date. Use your discretion, if you think it may be out-of-date or not relevant, don't include it.

Always put your highest and most relevant qualifications at the top. If you have a degree/professional qualification, those should go at the top, followed by other qualifications and then your work based training.

TOP TIP

If you gained your qualifications over ten years ago, the dates/grades/school or college you attended are unnecessary. You also don't need to list each 'O'Level/GCSE/CSE/'A'Level – just write 'O Levels' or 'GCSEs' etc. If you have them, you may wish to write, *'including Maths and English.'*

Often, I find that clients with technical roles such as health and safety manager or roles that require a high level of training have numerous qualifications. In these circumstances it's fine to add an extra page just for them – it serves to highlight just how qualified you are.

TOP TIP

Avoid putting work based training that isn't relevant to the roles that you're applying for (unless they're formal qualifications). They won't help you get the job, and you'll only be wasting valuable space.

SECTION 5 - ADDITIONAL INFORMATION

This section is entirely discretionary. A recruiter won't use it as a measurement; it simply gives a more holistic view of you. People are under the illusion that you have to include an 'Additional Information' section e.g. hobbies and interests; you don't. You should only incorporate it if you have something to say that will enhance your application. For example, you should only list hobbies/interests which align with company values. Interviewers like applicants who:

- Are involved with charities
- Are involved with sports

- Are involved with 'clubs' e.g. running/painting/football/ Scouts/Guides/Brownies/Cadets etc.
- Are studying – further education
- Have a non-paid role outside their regular job e.g. school governor, councillor, non-executive director
- Are fluent in another language

TOP TIP

You should avoid the usual hobbies/interests that everyone *thinks* that they should write e.g. cinema/socialising/ reading/gym. Everyone does those, and they say nothing about you. It would be better to leave this section out and use the space to add more quality information in other parts rather than waste space listing things that will not support your application.

If you do decide to include additional information:

- **Ensure that you can talk about it** - Whatever you write here has to be current, and you must be doing it now. I had one client who had written that he was a Scout leader, but when I quizzed him about it, he said that it five years ago, making it totally irrelevant now.

- **Tell the truth** – Don't put it if you don't do it. It's likely that whatever you put in this section will be explored during an interview. I've caught people lying when I've asked about their hobbies. I'll ask what the last film they saw was if they listed 'Cinema' as a hobby. I'm a massive film fan, and I know what's showing at the movies most of the time. If an interviewee can't answer me quickly or if they can't give me a recent film, I'll think they're lying.

That goes for 'reading' too. People like to list reading as a hobby, yet when I ask them what they're currently reading or who their favourite author or genre is, they frequently can't answer. Lying about your hobbies and interests and getting caught will throw everything else you've said into question, which can mean that you fail an otherwise excellent interview.

OTHER ADDITIONAL INFORMATION

- **Clean driving license** – Only include this information a recruiter asks for it.

You should **NOT** include any of the following:

- **Children/marital status** – Employers used to use it in their decision-making process e.g. more unscrupulous employers may not have wanted to employ women who had children because they thought they would take too much time off work to look after them.

- **Nationality** – As long as you have the right documentation to be able to work in the UK, then your nationality is irrelevant (although being able to speak English may be a prerequisite for the role).

- **Date of Birth** – As I've already mentioned, it's now illegal in the UK to discriminate on the grounds of age. Therefore, you do not need to include it on your CV.

- **Referees** – So many people write *'References available on request'* at the bottom on their CV. There's no need to state the obvious; it's a line that you can use for something more productive. You also don't need to waste space giving the names and contact details of your referees (unless they are explicitly asked for). If you're successful at interview, I'll guarantee that good companies will ask you for them as most job offers are conditional upon receiving two acceptable references.

- **Picture – ABSOLUTELY NOT!** In the UK, we don't use photographs on CVs. Recruiters don't like them due to the potential for discrimination e.g. a candidate could claim that the company rejected their application because of their ethnicity, sex, age, etc. rather than their ability to do the job. Other countries are different; therefore, if you're applying for roles outside the UK, it would be a good idea to research the accepted 'photograph' rule for the country the where the vacancy is based.

SCHOOL/UNIVERSITY/COLLEGE LEAVERS

Obviously, if you're a school/college/university graduate, it's unlikely that you'll have much relevant job information to include on a CV. Therefore, it's important to embellish your other non-work related achievements:

- If you've had a part-time job, you should obviously incorporate it under 'career history'. Explain what you did including your key responsibilities/duties and what you achieved within that role (no matter how small). Include things like, cash management, prioritisation, organisation, dealing with customers, relationship management, etc.
- You must include an extended 'Additional Information' section, providing information on clubs and activities that you are involved with. Here are some examples of what you could incorporate:
    - Scouts/Guides/Cadets
    - Duke of Edinburgh Awards
    - Sports e.g. football/netball/hockey/running etc.
    - Painting/drawing/design/IT
    - Ballet/dance/drama/arts

- Working with young people or charities
- Travelling
- Languages you are fluent in

This list is not exhaustive. Outline any achievements you've had in the course of your activities including qualifications, badges, certificates and a little around the key skills you needed to obtain them.

- You should also consider attaching a Personal Statement (see Chapter 6 for more information). A Personal Statement will give you the opportunity to tell the recruiter about the type of person you are, the skills and attributes that you have that make you suitable for their role and organisation.

TOP TIPS FOR COMPLETING YOUR CV

- Try to keep it to two pages. However, initially, you could write a much longer CV containing everything you've done and edit it down to two pages based on the requirements for each different role you apply for.

- You may want to write two or three different CV's matching the skills/experience required for various jobs.

- Don't write 'CURRICULUM VITAE' at the top. Everyone knows what the document and you only two pages, so don't waste the space.

- Write in the third person i.e. do not use 'I,' 'me,' 'my,' 'mine,' 'we,' etc.
- Don't include your opinion e.g. hardworking, trustworthy, dedicated, etc.
- Use typeface Arial pt 10 or 11 or Calibri pt 11.
- If you have a lot of qualifications, list them on a separate page.
- Make sure your CV is well laid out – easy on the eye.
- If printing paper, use quality paper.
- Check for typos, errors – ask someone else to check it
- Be truthful.
- **MAKE SURE IT'S ACHIEVEMENT FOCUSSED and ...**
- **TAILOR IT TO THE ROLE!**

CHAPTER 4 – SOCIAL MEDIA

"There are many things of which a wise man might wish to be ignorant."

(Ralph Waldo Emerson)

'Social Media' is a section that I've only recently added to our workshops due to the massive rise in social media. The 'face' that you present to the world, not only when you're job hunting but in general, is more important than ever, as it's incredibly easy for prospective employers to view our social media. Once something is 'out there' it's tough to get it back, and it could be years before something unprofessional that you post now, comes back to haunt you.

You're kidding yourself if you think that a prospective employer and recruitment consultants won't Google you and check out your social media. Therefore, it's incredibly important to do a complete review *before* you start your job search.

REVIEW YOUR SOCIAL MEDIA

1. **Facebook** - Take a critical look at your profile. Remove any posts that you could classify as discriminatory or that make you look anything less than professional. Take off any pictures that show you in uncompromising positions or that show you as a 'party animal'. Delete any negative comments you may have made about your current employer, colleagues or anything that you could construe as being discriminatory or overtly political.

   If you don't want to alter your Facebook content, then go to the settings section and completely lock down your profile so that no-one other than your friends can see your feed. Once you've done that, make sure that you test it to make sure it's working and keep checking it at regular intervals, as Facebook are notorious for allowing settings to slip. If you decide to adjust your settings rather than delete inappropriate material, be aware that there are ways to get around it. If in doubt, and by far the safest option, is to delete everything inappropriate/unprofessional.

2. **Twitter, Tumblr, Instagram, etc.** - Again, make sure that you go through your history and delete anything that you

wouldn't want a prospective employee to see. Removing unwanted information may be a little more difficult, depending on the media.

3. **LinkedIn** – This is social media for the business world and you should only post information on here that is professional – absolutely nothing personal. If you have a picture of yourself on your profile (and you must), it should show you in a professional light i.e. no pictures from a night out, holding a glass of wine, wearing your holiday clothes or with your partner/friend(s).

You need to be ruthless when you review your social media because the way that you present yourself to the wider world is how an employer will see and judge you. They will not consider recruiting someone has posted anything inappropriate or unprofessional.

In short, **if in doubt, take it out!**

EMAIL ADDRESSES

The email address you use is also vital to presenting yourself in a professional manner and again, should not contain anything inappropriate or unprofessional. It's placed at the top of your

CV so is one of the first things a recruiter sees. Practically every recruiter I talked to raised poor email addresses as an example of what not to do when you're job hunting.

If you have an email address that isn't professional, get another one for job hunting purposes. Your internet provider will often allow more than one email address with your contract. Alternatively, many online providers will allow you to order an email address completely free of charge e.g. Gmail, Outlook, Yahoo, etc.

If you're finding it hard to think of an appropriate name, use your name or your initials. If you can't get your name, don't embellish it with your age or year of birth, as this will give information that you shouldn't include in an application and that could be classed as discriminatory (we talked about age discrimination earlier). Find another way to personalise it by using your street name, your mother's maiden name, your middle name, etc. Just make sure that whatever you decide to go with isn't contentious in any way or will make you look unprofessional.

CHAPTER 5 - EFFECTIVE JOB SEARCH

"Dreams don't work unless you do."

There are so many different places find jobs now, gone are the days when you only looked in the local newspaper or contacted a local recruitment consultant. Since the last recession, job hunting has become much more diverse. Therefore, utilising a combination of different job sources is essential.

Job hunting is front loaded i.e. most of the work is up front. For example, you have to create your CV and then register with online sites, write your LinkedIn profile, register and meet with recruitment consultants, etc. However, once you've done the hard work, it's all relatively easy to maintain.

In this Chapter, we'll look at where to find the right job including:

- On-line Job Sites
- Job Centres
- Employment Agencies/Consultancies
- Newspapers/Trade Press
- Company Websites
- Speculative Applications
- Networking
- Using LinkedIn

I've also incorporated sections on how to apply for jobs, how to create covering letters that will get you noticed and how to complete application forms.

ON-LINE JOB SITES

There are so many job sites now that some clients find it quite overwhelming choosing the ones that will give the best results. I've worked with clients using the majority of the generic job sites; the following is a list of the most frequently used based on their feedback. Professional/career specific job sites are covered later. (N.B. I'm not necessarily recommending these sites, as I haven't used all of them personally):

Generic Job Sites (management and non-management)

- www.totaljobs.com – Great for all types of roles as it pulls through advertisements from career-specific websites as well as local and national newspapers and magazines.
- www.reed.co.uk
- www.indeed.co.uk
- www.monster.co.uk – Not quite as good as the previous three for professional or management roles but worth a look.

Non-management Job Sites

- www.kellyservices.co.uk – Especially useful for hourly paid roles including office administration, shop work, sales and junior management positions.
- www.jobsite.co.uk - All types of hourly paid and junior management positions.
- www.pertemps.co.uk

Management Job Sites

- www.glassdoor.co.uk – This is a great site which again pulls together roles from lots of different sources. It also has useful information on a range of job-related topics.
- www.michaelpage.co.uk – Michael Page is a recruitment consultancy that is country wide and manages jobs across a range of disciplines.
- www.hays.co.uk – Similar to Michael Page.

There are, of course, many more job sites available. However, the ones I've listed consistently advertise a diverse range of roles and are relatively easy to navigate.

USING ON-LINE JOB SITES

There are a few simple guidelines to follow to make the most out of using online job sites:

USING ON-LINE JOB SITES

1. **Register with each website and upload your CV** - Many recruiters subscribe to online job sites (it's one of the ways that sites generate income in addition to paid advertising) and will set up comprehensive searches to find people with the skills, experience, and qualifications they require to fill their vacancies. It's very cost efficient for them.

   - When uploading your CV, only leave one method of contact on there. Don't include your address, telephone number, *and* email address – you wouldn't put all that information on social media so why would you put it on a job site? Just put your telephone number and email address. You may also wish to put your location, but definitely not your whole address.

   - When a recruiter sets up a search, they enter a list of

keywords (usually essential skills and qualifications) required for the role. The site's software will then search CVs picking up those that contain the keywords. Therefore, if there are skills, experience or qualifications that you haven't listed in your CV, find a place to write them (any blank space will do) using keywords only, then disguise them by changing their colour to white. That way, they won't be actually 'seen' on the page, but they will be picked up by the trackers during a search.

- Update something on your CV every week (even if it's something small) and upload it again. When you do that, it puts your CV back to the top of the list. Recruiters often search by upload date (as they often only want to see candidates who are new to the market). Therefore, if you change something small and upload it again each week; you'll always remain at the top of the list.

2. **Use their advanced job search engines** – Most sites provide advanced job search features where you can be very specific about your requirements. You can search by:
   - Job Title (try different ones as job titles vary between companies)
   - Location
   - Salary
   - Full Time/Part Time

- Permanent/Contract/Interim

3. **Set up an email job alert** – Again, most sites offer this option. Once you enter your criteria, whenever a role that matches becomes live, you will receive an email. You may wish to limit the number of emails you receive, especially when registered with a few different sites; as you can become inundated. Most sites allow the option to get emails daily or weekly; I recommend opting for weekly.

4. **You can apply for roles online** – Applying online is very easy, simply follow the instructions provided. You'll need a good covering letter (explained later in this chapter) and your *tailored* CV. Even if the instructions say that a cover letter is optional, you should always include one. Some recruiters pre-sift from the covering letter alone and don't even read the CV initially, so it's always important to include one. Depending on the recruiter, you may be required to complete an application form which we'll look at later in this chapter.

5. **Manage your applications** – You'll be able to see what you've applied for and when within the 'member's area.'

6. **PRINT A COPY OF ALL APPLICATIONS** - Make sure that you always keep a copy of the job advertisement, the CV and covering letter for each application you make. Not keeping them is one of the biggest mistakes that job seekers make.

When you start a job search in earnest, you may find that you don't always hear any news for a few weeks. Therefore, if you don't keep a record, it's easy to forget what you've applied for, potentially causing embarrassment when you finally get the call for an interview. It never ceases to amaze recruiters when candidates turn up for an interview and say, *"What job am I here for again?"* It seems unbelievable, but it happens with frightening regularity!

You also need to make sure that you take the correct copy of your CV with you to the interview. By making a copy of each application, you'll ensure that silly mistakes are minimised. You can't afford to give a recruiter any reason, no matter how small, to reject you.

JOB CENTRE PLUS

I'm not going to focus too much on the Job Centre, as I'll be honest; none of the hundreds of people I've helped with their career have ever got a role through them. However, for completeness, I didn't want to leave it out.

Here's what you can expect from Job Centre Plus:

- They are not ideal for professional and management roles.

- They are suitable for hourly paid work such as warehouse operatives, shop workers, administrators, telesales, etc.
- They are a good place to look for voluntary jobs.
- They do provide advice and support to help you find work, especially if you've been out of work for a while.
- They're useful if you're a lone parent, have a disability, leaving school/college or are over 50.
- You can search the advertised jobs online at http://www.direct.gov.uk/en/Employment/Jobseekers/index.htm

NEWSPAPERS/PROFESSIONAL JOURNALS

Newspapers and professional journals now operate their job sections on similar lines to dedicated online job sites. Many have areas where you can register, apply and manage your applications. Here are some examples of media that have online job sections:

- Local Press - Ideal for 'hourly paid', non-professional/non-management roles and 'trade' roles e.g. shop assistants, warehouse operatives, plumbers, electricians, telesales, etc.
- National Press, for example:
    - The Guardian
    - The Times
    - The Independent
- Professional Journals including:

- Inside Housing
- Marketing Week
- People Management
- The Lawyer
- Hotel Business
- PR Week

Choose the ones that are pertinent to you and add them to your list to check on a regular basis.

RECRUITMENT CONSULTANCIES/AGENCIES

Working with consultants requires some degree of persistence, an understanding of what they will/won't do for you and knowing how to manage them effectively. Often, candidates will tell me that they're tired of getting nowhere fast with consultants, and they want to stop using them altogether. I usually find the reason they aren't getting the results they expected is because they simply aren't managing the candidate/consultant relationship.

In this section, I'll explain how to handle your relationship with consultants to get the best results. It's a mistake not to use them, even if you've had an unfortunate experience in the past. Not all consultants are the same and the agency/consultancy that you decide not to register with may have your perfect role. They should form an integral part of your job search activities.

RECRUITMENT CONSULTANCIES VS AGENCIES

There is a difference between recruitment consultancies and agencies. Consultancies tend to handle higher level professional, management and senior management roles. Agencies tend to manage hourly paid and junior management vacancies and while they both operate on similar principles, how they go about it can be quite different.

HIGH STREET AGENCIES

Agency recruitment consultants (often referred to as 'High Street Agencies'), are typically highly target driven and tend to have strict KPIs (Key Performance Indicators or targets) to hit. They have goals based on activities such as the number of:

- Business development calls made
- New vacancies secured
- Candidate interviews
- Placements made

They are likely to have a high turnover of positions, filling them relatively quickly. Here are some examples of the types of posts that an agency may manage:

- Warehouse operatives
- Office administrators/secretaries
- Drivers

- Shop workers
- Labourers
- Telesales
- Sales representatives
- Lower level professional roles such as accounts officers, HR officers/administrators, etc.
- Team leaders/departmental managers

See 'how to choose the right agency' for more information on selecting the right agencies for you.

RECRUITMENT CONSULTANCIES

The more boutique or higher level recruitment consultants usually have fewer roles than a typical high street agency and will work predominantly with professional and management positions at all levels. They may:

- Focus on a particular profession e.g. accountancy, or
- Deal with a particular sector e.g. manufacturing, or
- Cover a specific location e.g. North West.

Often, the types of roles they work with may be broken down still further. For example, they may:

- Deal with a particular level within a profession, sector or location e.g. junior/middle/senior/executive/board director.

- Focus on either interim/temporary/contract roles or permanent positions.

While their recruitment consultants will usually also have targets, they don't tend to be as strict or have as many as agencies (although that's not the case with some of the larger, national businesses) this enables them to build better relationships with their clients and candidates. Also, the roles that they manage tend to be more complex and require more work than a typical agency vacancy. Their targets are usually based on the number of placements they make and the revenue they generate.

ALL RECRUITMENT CONSULTANTS ARE SALES PEOPLE!

What you have to remember about all recruitment consultants is that they are essentially sales people. Most operate on a commission basis, which means that they have a low base salary and receive commission payments related to their targets, as an incentive.

Regarding what a company has to pay for the services of a consultancy or agency, it can range from anything between 8% of a placement's first year's salary (usually for hourly paid roles) to up to 50%+ on headhunted executive/board level positions. If we take a conservative example of a 25% placement fee (25-30% is about the norm) on a salary of £70,000, that works out at £17,500. If the consultant gets 10% commission, they will receive £1,700 for just that one placement.

The point of me sharing this with you is to emphasise that *it's in their interest place you.* The downside is that they will usually look for the quickest placements, which usually means, *'square peg, square hole.'* Therefore, if you're looking for a change of career without apparent experience in that field, don't expect to be placed as quickly as you might if you were looking for the same role/job title, or for a promotion within the same profession.

HOW TO CHOOSE THE RIGHT CONSULTANCY/AGENCY

There are a large number of agencies and consultancies available. The following is a list that I've compiled from the feedback I've received from my clients. Again, I must add a caveat here; I am not personally recommending or vouching for any of these companies, as I haven't worked with many of them personally.

1. **Hourly paid employment (non-management)** - If you're looking for non-management/junior management or hourly paid work whether full time/part time, permanent/ temporary, try high street agencies. Some of the big names include:

- Pertemps
- Forrest Recruitment
- Manpower

- Reed
- Blue Arrow
- Adecco

Many smaller, local agencies may cover your location and deal with many different types of roles at all levels. Use Google to find them or ask friends/colleagues for recommendations. I'd suggest you always go with recommendations as people don't usually make them unless they've had a good experience or know someone who has.

2. **Professional/management roles** – As well as the large national consultancies, there are also many good, smaller boutique ones that may suit your needs better. Again, ask for recommendations from other people in your profession or sector.

   Here are some of the larger, national companies:

- Michael Page
- Hays
- Robert Half
- Robert Walters

TOP TIP

Another good tip for finding the right consultancy is to go to a generic online job site such as www.totaljobs.com and type in the name of the job you require. You'll be able to see clearly which agencies/consultancies are managing those kinds of roles in your area. Even if they don't have a vacancy advertised that's exactly right for you, you should consider contacting and registering with them anyway.

WORKING WITH CONSULTANTS

1. **Meet the consultant face to face** (wherever possible) – I can't stress enough how important it is to build a good relationship with consultants. If they like you, and you have a good rapport with them, they are much more likely to think of you when they have a suitable role. If they haven't met you face to face, they'll be less 'bought in' to you and aren't likely to contact you.

   If you and the consultant are both in different locations, and it isn't feasible to meet face to face, then a Skype or Bluejeans (business video conferencing) interview may be preferable - see 'Skype/Bluejeans Interviewing' in Chapter 6 for more information.

2. **If they don't want to meet you, move on** - If a consultant doesn't want to meet with you, especially if you're a manager/professional, it's unlikely that they'll help you. When you call to introduce yourself, if they say, *"Just send your CV over, and I'll get back to you"* that should be a red flag. By all means, send your CV; however, be aware that it's unlikely that

you'll hear back from them. You shouldn't worry about it, move on to the next.

3. **Dress professionally** - A big complaint that consultants have is when candidates turn up for meetings wearing jeans or dressed too casually. That's simply not acceptable and yet for some reason, many candidates think it doesn't matter. When you meet with a recruitment consultant, you should treat it like you would any first interview, because that's exactly what it is, an interview. You wouldn't (or shouldn't) turn up at a job interview wearing jeans, so why would you do that when you meet a consultant? What you wear speaks volumes about your professionalism, so make sure you dress appropriately.

4. **Do your preparation** – A good recruitment consultant will want to know about your skills, experience, and qualifications to be able to match you to the right roles. Therefore, *you should prepare in the same as you would for any other face to face interview.* It's not acceptable to meet with a consultant without being able to talk through your CV and achievements.

5. **Consultants will market you** – Make a list of the companies you'd like to work for and give it to consultants (although you shouldn't give the same company names to more than one consultant to avoid duplication). Good ones will contact those companies on your behalf (provided that they agree with your

choices), especially if you're looking for senior management or professional roles.

6. TOP TIP **Don't rely on them calling you** - You *must* schedule a time to call them weekly or at the very least bi-weekly. Just because you're on their register and may have been for a while, it doesn't mean that you'll be top of their list when a suitable role comes in. It doesn't work like that.

   Some of my senior clients often get quite upset about this. They are so used to people running around after them that they think consultants should do it too. Unfortunately, that's not always the case. Consultants will tend to pick the phone up to a candidate they've just put the phone down from rather than search through their candidate bank.

   If you keep in constant contact with your consultants (I don't mean pestering them, but making well timed, quick calls once a week or so), you'll be at the forefront of their mind when a new, suitable role does come in.

7. **Always take their call** – Quite often recruitment consultants will withhold their number, and it may show on your phone as 'No Caller ID' or 'Unknown'. If you don't usually pick up those types of calls, I suggest that you do for the duration of your job search. If a consultant can't get hold of you first time, they may

move on to the next person on their list, and the opportunity could be lost.

If you're busy when the call comes in, make sure you ring them back as soon as possible, THAT DAY! Most consultants work late, so no matter how late it is, always call them back. Even if they don't answer, leave a message, at least, they'll know you're keen. It's rare that a consultant will attempt to call you again if you haven't bothered to return their initial call unless they are desperate for your skills/experience.

8. **Check consultancy/agency websites for roles** – If you see something advertised that you think would be suitable, don't wait to be called; ring the consultant immediately. Don't be offended if they haven't contacted you; they are probably dealing with hundreds of candidates at any one time, which is why *you* should keep in regular contact with them.

9. **Register with more than one** – Register with at least five agencies/consultancies to expand your chances of finding the right role. You never know, the one agency/consultancy that you *don't* register with may have your dream job.

10. **UK eligibility to work** – It's likely that you will be asked to provide evidence of your eligibility to work in the UK before a consultant works with you. It's a legal requirement in the UK, so don't forget to take it with you if you're meeting them face to

face or provide a copy promptly upon request.

11. **Log your calls** – When you've registered with a few consultants it's important to keep a record of who you speak to, the date and what you discuss, otherwise, it could get confusing. Use the contact spreadsheet in the 'Additional Resources' section at the back of the book or sign up at **www.yourdreamjob.co.uk** to receive a Microsoft Excel spreadsheet directly into your inbox.

12. TOP TIP **Don't disappear!** (Consultants call it 'radio silence'). If you change your mind or need some time to make a decision, be honest. They are realists; they know that things change and that you probably have 'live' roles with other consultancies/agencies. They will have much more respect for you if you're truthful and behave in a professional manner.

Keeping them informed of what's going on and your thought processes gives them the opportunity to manage their clients' expectations. They've heard it all before, and they always know something's wrong when a candidate 'disappears' and stops returning their calls.

Be aware that they do 'blacklist' candidates who act unprofessionally and regularly share their blacklists with consultants in other companies. You wouldn't necessarily know that you're on their blacklist either, as they will probably still accept your calls; however, they won't take any action or actively work on your behalf.

TOP TIP

Beware of companies contacting you and asking for money to market you/help you find a job. A company did this to my friend, Sharon, recently. A company called her after she had put her CV on a career website and offered to help her find a job. She rang me after their call, and I told her to go and meet with them if she wanted to, but under no circumstances should she part with any money. She went to see them and after a two-hour meeting their 'sales person' (although they didn't introduce themselves as such) explained how they could help her find her next job for the cost of, *"Only a few days' pay."* Following my advice, she said, *"Thanks, but no thanks"* and left.

YOU SHOULD NEVER HAVE TO PAY SOMEONE FOR HELPING YOU TO FIND A ROLE unless it's through a legitimate outplacement/career management company who are upfront with you about costs. No ethical company would try to manipulate you into buying their services and tempt you to a meeting under false pretences. If you get a call like Sharon did, always ask upfront how much their services will cost. If they are evasive and won't give you a straight answer, don't take it any further. Politely refuse and end the call.

HEADHUNTERS

Headhunters typically recruit professional, technical, senior management and board director roles. The headhunter will take a detailed description of the type of person that the client requires including skills, experience, qualifications, personality fit, etc. They will then research and compile a list of people currently doing the same or a similar role within competitor organisations. They will then contact those individuals, initially to gain an understanding of whether they would be open to a more in-depth conversation. The roles that headhunters handle are not always advertised.

Alternatively, the client may provide the headhunter with a list of names of individuals that they would like approached on their behalf. Headhunters will rarely reveal the identity of their client until the candidate is at interview stage.

If you get a call from a headhunter, even if you aren't looking for a job, you should always call them back and establish a good relationship with them. You never know when you may need them in future. If you aren't looking at that moment but know someone who is or may be open to a conversation, give them the details of your contact. That's an excellent way to build relationships.

SPECULATIVE APPLICATIONS

Applying directly to the companies that you'd like to work for is a great way find a new job. Recruiters like speculative applications because it's a cost-effective way to recruit as they don't have to pay advertising or consultancy fees, plus they get someone who is already motivated to work for them.

How to make speculative applications:

1. Make a list of the companies where you would like to work.

2. Send your CV speculatively through their online application process. If that option isn't available, research the recruitment contact information on their website and call to find out the name of the person to whom you should send your application. It's always better to get a name rather than just sending something to a generic email address with a 'Dear Sir/Madam' salutation.

3. Email your speculative application, the email itself acting as the covering letter (I discuss covering letters later in this chapter) and attaching your CV. Another great way of getting a recruiter's attention is to send a paper copy of your letter and CV. So few people send letters these days. Therefore, your application will stand out for the right

reasons. Remember to use good quality paper, not cheap photocopy paper.

4. Make sure that you clearly state your key skills and achievements in your covering letter.

Many companies advertise their roles through their website; therefore, you should consider registering with them (where possible) and add their sites to your daily action plan, checking them at least once a week.

TOP TIP

Always follow up an email application, whether it's speculative or not. Leave it a couple of days after sending and phone to ensure that it's been received. Don't forget to ask when you can expect to hear something. The reason for calling them is two-fold:

1. It shows that you are motivated and keen to work at their company.
2. You will know if they've received your application as are often be glitches with online applications, so it's always a good idea to check.

COVERING LETTERS

Covering letters are an important part of the self-marketing process. It's your opportunity sell yourself further, allowing you the opportunity to show a little more of your personality than you would in your CV. Therefore, if you have the option to attach a covering letter, you should always do it.

I met with a recruitment consultant recently, and we were discussing the content of this book. He said, *"Jo, please put something your book about covering letters. I can't tell you how frustrated I get when I receive a poor covering letter. I use the covering letter more than the CV now for pre-sifting – I sometimes don't even read the CV - so I get annoyed when it's poorly written. Another bug bear is where the candidate has clearly used a template, and they haven't edited it properly, sending it littered with mistakes. Also, I can't tell you how many times people get my name wrong, or shorten it. For goodness sake, if they can't even get my name right, well there's no way they're getting through to one of my clients, their application goes straight in the 'no' pile!"*

WRITING COVERING LETTERS

- Always write in the FIRST person – That means that you *can* include 'I,' 'me,' 'my,' 'we,' 'us.' However, minimise the use of the word 'we' as it implies that your achievements are as the result of a team effort rather than your own work.

- **Tailor it to the role**. Review the job description, person specification, and company's competencies (if possible) and adapt your letter to their requirements.
- Cut and paste from your CV where appropriate. Use your 'achievements', but do this sparingly; you don't want to replicate your entire CV!
- Be careful if you're overwriting an existing letter or using a template. You *must* double check that you've not made any mistakes and left any unwanted information from a previous application.
- Use your Power Words (as discussed Chapter 3).
- Use typeface Arial pt 10 or 11 or Calibri pt 11.
- Keep it relatively short; the equivalent of one side of A4 paper.
- Make sure it's well laid out and easy on the eye.
- If printing hard copies, use quality paper.
- Check for typos, errors – ask someone else to check it.
- Tell the truth.
- If emailing your application, start with 'Dear Name' or 'Dear Sir/Madam' and always end with, 'Kind regards' – DO NOT

write, *"Hi"* even in an email.

- The correct endings if you're sending a paper copy:
- Start with 'Dear Sir/Madam' end with 'Yours faithfully.'
- Start with 'Dear Name' end with 'Yours sincerely.'
- Address the letter to the contact mentioned in the advert where one there is one. Never shorten names and make sure that you get the recruiter's name right. If you don't, your application will usually be disregarded straight away.
- Quote the reference (if available) and where you saw the role advertised.
- Use a polite and positive ending.
- If you are emailing your application, don't attach the covering letter, it should form the email itself with the CV attached.
- And I'll say it again for emphasis - **MAKE SURE YOU TAILOR IT TO THE ROLE!**

I've included sample covering letters in the 'Additional Resources' section at the back of the book.

USING LINKEDIN

The use of LinkedIn has skyrocketed over the last few years. LinkedIn is the business equivalent of Facebook – but don't get the two confused. It's not a place to post what you had for breakfast or how drunk you were at the weekend. However, it is a fantastic way of letting your network and prospective employers know that you're looking for your next role. It's also a great source for finding vacancies, advertised in the jobs section as well as in specific groups.

If you don't already have a LinkedIn account, I suggest you get one quickly. It should be the very first thing you do after writing your CV. I will guarantee that whenever you call a recruitment consultant, as soon as you tell them your name and before you've even had a chance to start the conversation, they will have pulled your details up on LinkedIn.

The following are guidelines on how to set up your profile on LinkedIn, how to search for relevant roles and getting the best out of using the site.

HOW TO SET UP YOUR PROFILE ON LINKEDIN

1. Complete your CV before you register on LinkedIn – that will make building your profile so much easier.
2. Go to http://www.linkedin.com and set up an account.

3. Start to build your profile, by literally copying and pasting information from your CV into the corresponding sections.

4. As you start to build your profile, LinkedIn will recommend people to connect with based your current/previous employers. Click on the 'connect' button below LinkedIn's recommendation to send an invitation.

5. You can also search for and connect with people you know by typing their name into the search engine at the top of the page.

WHERE TO FIND JOBS ON LINKEDIN

Once you have built your profile and started to connect with people, start looking for suitable roles:

1. Search for relevant jobs by clicking the 'Jobs' tab and using the advanced search facility.

2. Sign up for their automatic job search emails.

3. Apply for suitable roles in the same way that you would for other job sites.

4. Join groups that are relevant to you. Not all recruiters advertise their roles in the 'jobs' section. Instead,

they use specific groups. Advertising within job-specific groups is a fantastic, cheap way for them to hit their target market directly. Remember to adjust your settings when you join a group, otherwise, you may find that they bombard you with daily updates. Instead, choose to receive a weekly digest.

WRITING UPDATES AND POSTS

Writing good quality updates and posts are great ways to get noticed, to enhance your profile and increase your network. 'Updates' are the equivalent of 'posts' on Facebook, they provide the reader with general information about what you are doing. 'Posts' give you the opportunity to share interesting information and are similar to writing a blog post. Here are some guidelines for getting the most out of your updates and posts:

1. **Give regular but POSITIVE updates** – Updates could include information about what about what you're doing or general observations on news stories. I often post updates when I've delivered public speaking sessions as it helps raise my profile and it keeps my followers informed of my activities. Never whine or moan if you find yourself out of work, no-one wants to hear that, and they'll be less inclined to help you. Also, don't beg for help finding a job, *'needy*

smells' and people will be less likely to support you if that's the impression you're projecting.

2. **Keep upbeat** - Keep updates light and professional.

3. **Write regular updates** – It keeps you in your readers' minds.

4. **Write thought-provoking posts** - If you like writing; it's a great way to get noticed in the right way.

Even the most technophobic of people can set up a LinkedIn profile. However, if you require a little extra help, there are lots of tutorials available either within LinkedIn or on YouTube. Visit my LinkedIn page if you're looking for a good example of a completed profile. Feel free to connect with me too. You can find my profile at https://uk.linkedin.com/in/jo-banks-738b4412.

NETWORKING

Since the last recession, it's claimed people find more than 70% of new roles through their current network. It's quite a startling statistic and from what I've experience, it certainly seems to be true. Using your network is a fantastic way of discovering vacancies that haven't been advertised.

You may think, *"I don't have a network. I don't have many contacts."* That simply isn't true. Your network isn't limited to past and present work colleagues; it encompasses EVERYONE you know. For example, I was explaining the significance of utilising your network to a client. She was a Personal Assistant to the CEO of a large corporation, and her role had been made redundant due to the relocation of the Head Office. We discussed the importance of informing people in her network that she was looking for her next opportunity.

The next morning she did the school run, and one of the other mums asked if everything was OK because she didn't usually drop her child off. My client was explaining that her role had been made redundant, when the other mum exclaimed, *"Oh my husband is looking for a new PA! Let me have a chat with him."* Her husband was the owner of a large local business, and it turned out that he was indeed looking for a new PA.

Within a week, my client had been interviewed and had started in her new role. Had she not said anything to the other mum, she may never have even found out about the vacancy. The business owner was thrilled because he didn't have to go through a costly recruitment process and my client was happy because she managed to secure the perfect role with minimal effort. It was a win/win situation, both sides got what they needed with minimal effort.

HOW TO NETWORK EFFECTIVELY

I'm very well aware that networking can be daunting. After all, it's a large part of my job, but that doesn't mean that I like it or find it easy. It's important for me to network consistently as I receive the majority of business though the people who already know me or from their recommendations. I do no formal advertising, therefore, keeping my network flowing is crucial.

The following are guidelines for how to network effectively:

1. Make a list of every person you know.

2. Grade them one to three.
    - **One** is someone you know well, whom you are comfortable contacting for coffee/lunch.
    - **Two** is someone that you know reasonably well, but you may not have seen/spoken for a while. They could be a past colleague or even a customer/supplier with whom you have a good relationship.
    - **Three** would be someone (an acquaintance) whom you know, but not very well.

3. GET ON THE PHONE – Start ringing the 'ones' first.

    - Aim to call five people per day.
    - Call in the morning between 10.00 am and 12.00 noon if possible. I know that may be difficult if you're working

and if that's the case, plan to call at least two people during breaks.

- Call from a quiet place where you won't be interrupted.
- If possible, stand up while you're making calls at it will naturally add expression to your voice.
- Your intention should be to make people aware that you're looking for a job, not necessarily within their company. You're asking them to keep you in mind if they hear of something that may be suitable. After all, if they don't know that you're looking, they can't help.
- Be able to give an overview of the type of job you want.
- Be able to talk confidently about your key skills.
- **DON'T COMPLAIN ABOUT YOUR SITUATION AND KEEP POSITIVE.**
- Try and arrange to meet up with them face to face where you think it may be beneficial.
- Diarise callbacks and make sure that you follow through.
- Have your CV ready to send.
- Take regular breaks, do other activities between calls to clear your head.
- Use the 'Contact Spreadsheet' in the 'Additional Resources' section at the end of the book to log your activities; who you speak to, when and what you discuss.

If you do find it a little scary, think how you would feel if someone called you and asked for your help. Every single person I have this discussion with says that they wouldn't hesitate. Most people have a desire to help others; it's hardwired in our DNA, which is one of the reasons the human race has survived for so long. Keep that in the back of your mind when you make your calls.

TOP TIP

Buying someone a coffee or even lunch is a fantastic way to get that person to help you as it invokes the law of reciprocation i.e. when we do something for someone else, no matter how small, they feel obliged to do something for us. When I was setting up my business, I paid for countless coffees in return for copious amounts of free advice (worth the trade as far as I was concerned).

PLANNING YOUR JOB SEARCH

I'm hallucinating now that some of you may be feeling a little overwhelmed. It's usually at this point in a workshop that delegates start feeling a little panicky when they realise how much work they have to do. Please don't; what you need to do now is create an effective plan to pull everything together. If you have a detailed daily plan that you stick to, you are much more likely to achieve great results.

IF YOU'RE CURRENTLY *OUT* OF WORK...

If you do find yourself out of work, it's even more important to have a plan to ensure that you're making the most of the time you have available. There are a couple of patterns that I've observed with people out of work:

1. **'The Overachiever'** - This group of job seekers are either very output driven in everyday life or are inclined to panic/worry. Either way, they stop at nothing to get a new role; working day and night tirelessly until they secure something suitable. This group can feel particularly stressed/anxious and don't usually to take any time for themselves during their frantic search. However, almost without exception, they'll be back in work relatively quickly wishing that they'd done more with their time off.
2. **'The Procrastinator'** – This set of job hunters start with good intentions. For the first week or so, they do their CV, check the job sites regularly, register with a couple of agencies, however, things start to drift. After that initial spurt, they start to get up later and later and then they do the unthinkable; they start watching daytime TV. Whatever you do, NEVER turn on daytime TV, it's like a tractor beam, it sucks you in and before you know it, it'll be 3.30 pm, you'll still be in your PJs, and the kids will be coming home from school!

These individuals can suffer higher levels of anxiety and guilt. They know they should be doing their job hunting, but tell themselves, *"I'll do it later..."* or *"I'll just finish watching this programme and then I'll start..."* They feel overwhelmed, and it all seems too hard, so they end up doing nothing.

TOP TIP

If you're out of work, the very best way to carry out a productive job search is to dedicate approximately two hours a day, five days a week, preferably Monday to Friday, where you do nothing else. Do it between 10.00 am and 12.00 noon, I recommend this time because it's the optimum period for catching people at their desks if you're making calls and it also seems to be when individuals are at their most productive.

Plan this time in your diary as you would any important, immoveable meeting. You need to be sitting at your computer/laptop, at 10.00 am without fail, ready to work; doing this will train your brain to know that you're serious, and you are likely to achieve better results.

IF YOU'RE CURRENTLY *IN* WORK...

If you're currently in work, it's obviously not going to be possible to set aside two hours, five mornings a week, unless you work shifts. Therefore, you need to work a bit differently:

1. Initially, set some time aside one weekend to do your CV, register with the online job sites and complete your LinkedIn profile.
2. Make sure that time is immovable and that you won't be interrupted.
3. Set at least half an hour aside each evening (five days a week) to look for and apply for jobs online.
4. Schedule half an hour each weekday (utilise your breaks) to make your calls.
5. You may need to book time off work to go for meetings/interviews. However, often recruiters, including recruitment consultants, will be happy to see you out of hours, either before or after work.

DAILY ACTIVITY PLAN

Create a daily activity plan so that you use your time efficiently. Research has shown that *'what gets written down gets done'.* Therefore, having a plan that you stick to is important to get the most out of your job search.

Your plan should have a mixture of the activities I've detailed in this chapter e.g. you may wish to call three contacts and two recruitment consultancies, visit two job sites and apply for four jobs or any combination that suit you. There's a copy of a part completed 'Daily Activity Plan' in the 'Additional Resources' section of this book for guidance.

The following is a reminder of the job search activities that you may want to include in your daily action plan. Make sure you add numbers to each activity e.g. ring *three* consultants, etc.:

- Job Sites
- Job Centre Plus
- Newspapers/Professional Journals
- Recruitment Consultancies/Agencies
- Speculative Applications
- LinkedIn
- Networking

At the end of each job search session, mark off the things that you've completed/accomplished and plan your activities for the next day. That way, you won't waste time deciding what to do at your next session; you can hit the ground running. Without a plan, clients often find themselves feeling helpless and overwhelmed, not managing to achieve anything. Also, you'll be able to monitor your progress and see what's working (which you should do more of) and what's not (ditch it).

If you are currently out of work, once you have completed your hunt job session, make the most of the rest the day and take the afternoon/evening to do something you enjoy, guilt free. If that includes exercise, especially outdoors, then that's even better as it increases blood flow and releases endorphins which help lower cortisol (the stress hormone). So many clients tell me, *"I wish I'd spent more time doing things for the family and me while I was out of work. I feel like I've wasted so much valuable time and I may never get that opportunity again."* Don't let that be you!

CHAPTER 6 – ASSESSMENT TYPES & PREPARATION

"Fail to prepare, prepare to fail."

(Benjamin Franklin)

OVERVIEW OF ASSESSMENT TYPES

Currently, there are more recruitment assessment types than ever before. Interviews used to be the primary or only selection method and still remain the tool of choice for many recruiters. However, as competition is now increasingly fierce and the marketplace has more candidates than vacancies, many employers are turning to increasingly sophisticated methods in order to select the very best candidates in the most cost effective way.

During my research for this book, I interviewed freelance recruitment assessors currently working for large organisations. Therefore, the advice in this chapter not only comes from my expert knowledge of assessment tools but directly from those who are currently involved in marking them.

Companies tend to use freelance assessors to support a range of evaluation activities such as video interviews, telephone interviews, assessment centres, etc. The benefit of using external people is that they are impartial and mark answers according to strict guidelines, eliminating the chance of any bias. It's also cost effective to bring in additional, expert resource rather than employing additional permanent headcount.

The following is a list of the most popular selection methods which I cover in detail in this chapter:

- Application forms
- Personal statements
- Online testing
- Video assessment
- Interviews:
    - Telephone
    - Skype/ Bluejeans
    - CV based
    - Competency based
- Assessment Centres
- Presentations

PREPARATION IS KEY

The quote I used at the beginning of the chapter, *"Fail to prepare, prepare to fail"* sums it up nicely. One of the overriding reasons why candidates fail assessments, especially interviews and presentations, is a lack of preparation. Excessive candidate nerves can mainly be attributed to a lack of preparation. Candidates who do everything possible to prepare, usually find that their nerves, stress, and anxiety are automatically reduced as a result.

You know that the purpose of any assessment is to find out how your skills and experience match those required for the job – as well as your general 'fit' for the role and the company. I estimate that you can anticipate 80-85% of the questions you will be asked at an interview, so why on earth wouldn't you prepare?

When my clients go for an interview, I ask them to call me afterward so that we can review their performance and work on any development areas. If they say, *"That went really badly"* my first question is always, *"Did you do all your preparation as we discussed?"* Invariably, the answer is, *"No"* and we discuss what they need to do differently next time. For those who did do their preparation, I'll ask, *"Could you have done any more?"* Again, usually, the answer is, *"No"*. If that's the case, I tell them that the role or the company simply wasn't right for them, and they need to move onwards and upwards. Usually, something bigger and better will come along soon afterwards.

APPLICATION FORMS

Apart from the traditional CV and covering letter, application forms are still a favourite pre-sifting tool which is often automated. Many large companies and organisations receive hundreds of applications for a single vacancy and have, therefore, invested in computer software designed to manage bulk applications.

These programs will assess an application against certain essential criteria (keywords) for the vacancy e.g. qualifications, skills, experience, etc. If a submission contains information that matches the criteria, it will be highlighted to be reviewed further by an assessor. If it doesn't, it will automatically be rejected potentially without ever being viewed by a human.

COMPLETING ONLINE APPLICATION FORMS

Online applications can be a little trickier to complete than their paper counterparts. However, I've included guidance notes to ensure that you have the best chance of success:

COMPLETING APPLICATIONS FORMS

1. **Print a copy before you start to fill it in online** – Where possible, print a copy of the form and practise writing your answers on the copy before transferring them to the original online.

2. **Follow instructions carefully** – Many candidates tend to 'skim' read (usually because they're nervous) and, therefore, don't give the correct answer or too much/too little information.

3. **Jot down ideas before you start** – By doing this, you'll lessen your chances of making errors.

4. **Confine answers to the space provided** – Unless you get told that you can use an extra sheet, you should adhere to the area defined, ensuring that your answers are concise. I suggest you use the STAR format (which is described later in this chapter) to structure your answers where appropriate.

5. **Enter information accurately** - You should pay particular attention to dates, ensuring that they are correct. For some reason candidates often mistype dates.

6. **Fill in ALL sections** - As application forms are often scored, if you don't complete a section you may be missing out on

valuable points. Avoid jumping over parts thinking that you'll go back and fill in later, as you may forget, again potentially missing out on valuable points.

7. **Stick to the number of words stipulated** – When there is a word count you should stick to it. Anything you write over and above will not receive a score. If you don't reach the word count, it's unlikely that you will have answered the question thoroughly enough to achieve top marks.

8. **Use your achievements from your CV** - If you are asked competency based questions e.g. *"Give an example of when you have had to ..."* use the 'achievements' that you have listed on your CV. Copy and paste them if appropriate (although you may need to add a little extra information – remember to use the recommended word count).

   Where possible use the company's competencies to tailor your answers. Competencies are sometimes called 'Values' or 'Behaviours' and can usually be found on a company's website. There is more information on competencies later in this chapter.

9. **Check for typos/errors** – We can't always see our own mistakes, therefore, ask someone else with a good command of written English to check it for you. I realise that this isn't always possible especially if it's the kind of online form that won't let you go back once you've clicked 'NEXT.' If that's the case, take

the time to read each completed section carefully before clicking to the next page.

A way around this is to type your responses first in a word processing software program such as Microsoft Word or Apple's Pages, which will provide you with an accurate word count as well as highlighting any spelling and grammatical errors. Once you are happy with what you've written, copy and paste your answers into the application form.

10. **Make sure that your referees know about your application and are happy to support you** – It's common courtesy to inform your referees that a prospective employer may contact them.

11. **Send it to the right person** – If the application process isn't automated, take care to email your application to the right person and that you have spelled their name and address/email correctly.

12. **Complete it on time** – If your application is late, it will probably be rejected, no matter what your reason is for its late arrival.

13. **Keep a copy** – This is important, as you'll need it to refer to it should you be selected for an interview. Sometimes with online application forms, you aren't able to go back once you've pressed enter. In this case, use the Print Screen button on your keyboard [PrtScn] and paste [Ctrl V] the screen print into MS

Word, PowerPoint, Paint or an alternative software program. It may be a bit laborious, but it will be worth it.

Another benefit of saving copies of completed application forms is that you can use the same information for subsequent applications, thereby reducing re-work, saving time and energy.

HARD COPY APPLICATION FORMS

If you have a paper application form, make a copy of it and fill in the copy first. Once you're happy with your answers, transpose them onto the original. That way you'll minimise the chance of making a mistake. Again, ask someone else to read and check it for errors.

ONLINE TESTING

Online testing is an assessment instrument that's becoming increasingly popular. They're typically utilised as a pre-sifting tool or as part of an assessment centre. They test specific skills e.g. verbal, numerical, technical or your personality type using psychometrics. Psychometric testing is covered later in this chapter under 'Assessment Centres'.

COMPLETING ONLINE TESTS

1. **Read the questions carefully** – Candidates can tend to skim read questions instead of taking the time to read through them thoroughly, digesting all of the information. The quicker you read something, the more chance there is of you misreading it. Slow your pace down and read the questions out loud or write them on a piece of paper. Make sure you thoroughly understand what you are being asked for before answering. Remember in school when you were practising for exams and your teacher would say, *"Make sure you read and understand the question"*? The same principle applies here.

2. **Review your spelling** – Most candidates don't spend enough time checking their spelling; that indicates that you don't pay attention to detail. Reading your answers out loud as you type them can help you recognise errors.

3. **Check for grammatical errors** – Some candidates are so concerned about the content of their answers that they forget to follow the correct rules of grammar. Where competition is intense, recruiters are looking for reasons to filter out applicants. If you can't express yourself clearly in writing, there's less chance that you'll get through to the interview stage or pick up

the points you need in an assessment centre.

Write straightforward sentences that aren't too long or overcomplicated. Reread each sentence after typing it. Look for missing punctuation, sentence fragments, capitalisation errors, sentence run-ons or wordy sentences that you could interpret in different ways. Again, you may consider copying and pasting your answers into a word processing program which will automatically highlight any errors.

4. **Manage your nerves** – Nerves can affect concentration, resulting in a bad performance. I've included information on how to handle nerves in Chapter 7. In essence, make sure you eat something to give you energy, visualise performing well and think positively. Use the breathing exercise I've described and read each question carefully which will help take your mind off your nerves.

5. **Listen to your gut instinct** – Many candidates make the mistake of writing what they *think* the recruiter wants to hear rather than what *they* consider to be right. People can doubt themselves and end up not answering questions honestly. You must always be honest and go with your first gut instinct, that way if you don't get the job; you know that the position wasn't right for you.

VIDEO ASSESSMENTS

Video assessments (not to be confused with Skype interviews) are a relatively new assessment technique, increasingly used by larger organisations particularly for graduate and technical roles. They are predominantly another pre-sifting tool.

HOW VIDEO ASSESSMENTS WORK

You will be given a link by the recruiter that will take you through to a specially designed website where you will get asked a series of questions and your answers will be video recorded. Your answers are likely to be timed (usually around two minutes each). However, unlike a telephone or face to face interview, there won't be an interviewer there to prompt you if you aren't answering the questions thoroughly.

Once you log on to the system, you must be ready to start the interview as there's no going back. You should prepare for a video assessment in the same way as you would for a face to face interview using your key achievements in the STAR format (see 'Using the STAR format' later in this chapter), taking the company's competencies into consideration. Practise saying your achievements out loud as many times as possible before the assessment.

The interview will last for approximately 15-20 minutes and when completed, will be sent to an assessor for marking. The assessor will predominantly look for your thought processes and that you have answered the questions fully.

TOP TIP

Although assessors are explicitly told not to take account of how you look or the room is presented behind you, those things are a reflection of you/your standards and professionalism. Therefore, both you and the room should look neat and tidy. Remember that whatever you can see on the screen; the assessor can see! Position yourself in front of a blank wall if you're concerned about your surroundings.

TOP TIP

While you don't need to wear a suit, do make sure that you dress smart/casual (no PJs, no slogan T-shirts, inappropriate or dirty clothing). Comb your hair and make sure that you look presentable. Remember to look at the camera on your computer/laptop, not your own picture on the screen.

PERSONAL OR SUPPORTING STATEMENTS

Personal statements are required less frequently than other forms of assessment but can be requested to supplement your CV or application form. They should not be confused with the 'Summary

Statement' at the top of a CV (sometimes also called a 'Personal Statement').

Personal statements frequently form part of internal recruitment processes following organisational restructures where many of the affected employees have long service, and, therefore, the company already know their work history. The personal statement is a perfect way for the company to find out more about the individual, especially in areas such as motivation and aptitude for the new role. Personal statements are sometimes required for post-graduate positions where applicants are likely to have limited work experience.

PERSONAL STATEMENT CONTENT

Personal statements provide a chance for you to market your skills, experience and to outline your overall suitability for the role. The company will usually tell you how long your statement should be (up to one page of A4 is typical) and what they want you to cover. Read their guidelines carefully and take the time to plan the structure and content.

A typical statement would usually be structured in the following way:

1. An opening paragraph which starts with a strong statement explaining why you have decided to apply for the role.

2. Several middle paragraphs which outline your relevant experience, knowledge, skills and interests. You can use some of the achievements from your CV here and make sure that you refer to the company's competencies (where applicable).
3. A conclusion which sums up what you have to offer and why you think they should consider you for the role.

PERSONAL STATEMENTS FOR UNIVERSITY

Most universities ask for a personal statement and requirements can vary from between 500 to 5,000 words. They are particularly useful in this scenario because it's likely that applicants will have little relevant experience to include on a CV. Visit the university's website for clear guidelines on what to include as well as the suggested word count.

COMPLETING PERSONAL STATEMENTS

1. Ensure that you carefully read instructions – avoid skim reading as you may miss relevant points.

2. For job applications, refer to the job description and person specification and make sure that you write something for each of the essential skills required for the role.

3. Carefully plan out each section of your statement ensuring not only that you cover the key skills, but also the company's competencies (usually available on their website).

4. Write in the first person e.g. 'I,' 'me,' 'my,' 'we,' 'our,' etc.

5. Where a word count is stipulated, make sure that you stick to it. If you go over, you will only be marked up to the word count allowance. The assessor will disregard anything else. If you are significantly under the word count, it's likely that you haven't provided enough information.

6. Check it carefully for spelling and grammatical errors. Ask someone who has good written English language skills to read it for you as it's often difficult to recognise your own mistakes.

SITUATIONAL JUDGEMENT TESTS

Situational judgement tests are a type of psychological aptitude test designed to assess your judgement and decision making when solving problems in work-related situations. You will usually complete them online, without any strict time limits.

You will be given hypothetical and challenging scenarios that you could potentially face on a day-to-day basis in the role. In response to each situation, there will be more than one way deal with or solve the problem. They are usually presented in a multiple choice format and consist of up to 50 situations linked to the organisation's competencies.

Depending on the type of test, you will be required to do one of the following:

- Select both the most effective and the least effective response to the situation described.
- Pick only the most effective response.
- List the responses in order of effectiveness.

Situational judgement tests have become increasingly popular as assessment tools because they test softer job-related skills that other assessments are unable to measure. They examine practical intelligence and non-academic skills such as problem solving, decision making and interpersonal skills e.g. empathy and how you relate to others. They are frequently used in combination with knowledge-based tests to give a holistic view of a candidate's aptitude for a particular job.

PREPARATION

There is little preparation you can do for SJTs as they are designed to test your general knowledge, ability and life experience. However, I would recommend that you try some practise tests before completing the real thing. Some websites provide these free of charge. Experiment with few different ones as they do vary depending on the company/psychologist who's written them.

COMPLETING SJTS

1. Practise, practise, practise! The more practise you do, the easier the tests will be on the day.
   - Practising will allow you to identify patterns in your responses e.g. are you a team player or a leader.
   - Only use practise tests that have been designed by qualified Chartered Occupational Psychologists, that way you'll know you've been getting good, quality practise (the website should confirm the designer's qualifications).
2. Read the question thoroughly and only assign an answer after you've thought carefully about it.
3. Remember that you aren't being asked to judge whether an option is right or wrong, but to evaluate which one you consider being the best (and worst) option(s) available.
4. Don't make assumptions; you must base your responses only on the information provided.
5. When answering the questions, keep the company's competencies in mind and consider the type of role you're applying for and the qualities needed in that role.

6. SJTs aren't usually timed, however, if yours is; remember to keep a close eye on the time.

7. Answer ALL the questions. Avoid thinking that you'll go back to a question if you're not sure of the answer. Typically people who do that run out of time and aren't able to go back.

8. Ask the recruiter if they have any sample questions that you can use as practise.

TELEPHONE INTERVIEWS

You should prepare for telephone interviews in the same way as you would a face to face interview. The biggest mistake people make is to think that telephone interviews are less important than those conducted face to face and therefore, they don't put as much effort into their preparation.

TELEPHONE INTERVIEWS

1. **Use a landline** (where possible) – Quite often, the reception can be poor on a mobile phone. Using a landline should reduce any reception related problems.

2. **If you're in the car, pull over** – Don't conduct an interview

while you're driving. It's not professional, and you'll never be able to give the interviewer (or your driving) the attention they deserve. If you have to take the call while you're out, make sure that you're parked up in a safe place, at least five minutes before the interview start time.

3. **Use a quiet room where you won't be interrupted** – If you're at home and the family are around, ask them to go out for an hour during your call. There's nothing worse than having someone barge in on you when you're right in the middle of explaining the key aspects of your role.

4. **Remove any pets from the room** – This was a top tip from a recruitment consultant friend of mine. She said that it's incredibly annoying and off-putting (not to mention unprofessional) when a candidate stops an interview to pet their pooch!

5. **Stand up and walk around** – If possible, you should always stand up and walk around. *Motion creates emotion*; therefore, if you're on your feet, you'll be much more animated which you will reflect in your voice.

6. **Have the right information to hand** – You should have your CV, the job description, person specification, your key achievements in the STAR format, the company's competencies and your questions for them in front of you. The great thing

about telephone interviews is that the interviewer can't see you referring to your notes.

7. **Ensure responses are clear, concise and succinct** – If you've done your interview preparation i.e. you've practised saying your achievements in the START format, out loud numerous times, then this shouldn't be a problem. Keep answers short and to the point and avoid waffling.

8. **Pay extra attention to what the interviewer is asking** – When we can't see the other person, we obviously can't see their body language to know exactly what they mean (words are only 7% of our overall communication). Therefore, if you're unsure what the interviewer means, don't be afraid to ask for clarification or for the question to be repeated.

TOP TIP

9. **Know when to keep quiet** – In any interview, you should be aware when to keep quiet. Just because the interviewer is quiet when you've finished giving an answer does not mean that you have to fill the space with waffle! Know when to stop. If the interviewer is quiet on the phone, it usually means that they are writing notes; it's not a cue for you to keep talking. I've seen so many candidates ruin perfectly good answers because they don't know when to stop. Stick to your

STAR format and don't be tempted to add more to fill the silence, that's not your job, let the interviewer do that.

10. **Have your questions ready for them** – Prepare some intelligent questions to ask them. Examples are discussed later in the chapter.

11. **Remember to ask *"What happens next?"*** – Quite often candidates are so glad that the interview is over that they forget to ask what happens next. You should try to find out what the next stage will be before the end of the call.

SKYPE/BLUEJEANS INTERVIEWS

Many employers and recruitment consultants now use Skype or Bluejeans (business video conferencing) as a pre-sifting tool, before a formal face to face interview. It's especially useful where the candidate and assessor are based in different locations.

Again, you should prepare for a Skype interview as you would for a face to face meeting. However, I do have some top tips, which are very similar to those I outlined in the 'Video Assessment' section earlier in this chapter.

SKYPE INTERVIEWS

1. **Check your appearance** – Although it's not necessary to wear a suit, you should ensure that you look neat and professional. Wear a shirt/blouse and make sure that your hair is neat and tidy. DO NOT wear sportswear or anything revealing.

2. **Be mindful of your surroundings** – Even though the assessor shouldn't take the room behind you into consideration, if it is dirty, messy or you have inappropriate posters on the walls, it won't give a professional image. Position your computer/ phone/tablet in a way that you are in front of a blank wall. What you see on the screen is what the assessor can see.

3. **Have the right information at hand** – Have a copy of the job description, person specification, company's competencies, your CV, STAR format answers and your questions for them in front of you, so that you can refer to them quickly.

4. **Check that the technology is working** – There's nothing more frustrating for a recruiter than arranging time in their busy schedule to talk to a candidate, only to find that their Skype isn't working. Try it out with a friend beforehand so that you're ready to go at the allotted time.

5. **Look into the camera** – Candidates tend to look at the little

picture of themselves displayed on the screen rather than looking into the camera lens. Looking at your own picture appears very odd to the assessor, so make sure you address the camera rather than your own image.

FACE TO FACE INTERVIEWS

Face to face interviews are still an integral part of the recruitment process, and are relatively easy to prepare for if you know how.

In essence, there are two types of face to face interviews:

1. **CV based interviews** – Even though competency interviews are hugely popular, CV based interviews are still standard for both management and non-management roles. The interviewer may have some pre-prepared questions; however, usually they will just ask you to talk through your CV, asking pertinent questions as you go along.

TOP TIP

Although this type of interview is a little more ad-hoc and less structured than competency based interviews, **you should still prepare in the same way as you would for competency based interviews.**

The interview will last anything from half an hour to an hour and a half (the norm being around an hour) depending on the type of role and interviewer. The regular structure of an hour-long interview is:

- Opening by the interviewer - they provide information about the company and background on how the vacancy has arisen (5 minutes)
- The candidate talks through their CV with the interviewer asking pertinent questions (40 minutes)
- The candidate asks the interviewer their questions (10 minutes)
- Conclusion to interview including next steps (5 minutes)

2. **Panel/structured/competency based interviews** – This type of interview is typical for management, senior management, professional and graduate roles. Most large companies and public sector organisations use competency based interviews as their primary method of assessment for all vacancies.

   The difference between this style of interview and the CV based version is that every candidate receives the same set of questions. Each answer is marked giving a rating or score for the quality of the answer, according to strict criteria agreed during the interview design stage. The candidate with the highest overall score will usually be offered the role.

   There is a caveat here; often companies set a benchmark that must be reached before an offer can be made. For example, the benchmark may be 75 out of 100, therefore, if none of the candidates score 75 or more, they will all be rejected.

This type of assessment is appealing to recruiters because:

- It avoids 'face fits' i.e. giving the position to the person whom the interviewer favours, rather than based their merits.
- It helps prevent potential discrimination claims as there will be clear, recorded reasons to back up decision-making. It makes it harder for rejected candidates to build a claim against the company for discrimination based on their race, colour, religion, sex, disability, etc.

However, they do have their downsides:

- Where the interviewee is particularly nervous, they may not answer questions thoroughly enough to earn a high enough mark.
- It can be difficult to accurately test the candidate's 'personality fit' with the company/team. I've seen candidates placed in roles because they scored the highest at an interview. However, they didn't quite fit in with the rest of the team and subsequently ended up

leaving either by choice or force, within their probationary period.

A typical competency based interview lasts between one and a half and two hours. A one and a half hour interview is usually structured as follows:

- Opening by the interviewer who provides information on the company and how/why the vacancy has arisen (10 minutes)
- The interviewer asks the candidate competency based questions (60 minutes)
- The candidate asks the interviewer their questions (10 minutes)
- Conclusion to interview, including what happens next (10 minutes)

Competency based interviews also tend to form an essential part in Assessment Centres, which we'll talk about in more detail later in this Chapter.

HOW TO PREPARE FOR AN INTERVIEW

Preparing for any interview is relatively easy; however, it does require time and effort. The thing to remember when you do your preparation is that an interviewer isn't (or shouldn't be) trying to catch you out; they want to check that you have the right skills, experience, aptitude and behaviours to be successful in the role. It's like any test – you wouldn't turn up for an exam without having done your revision/preparation, so why would you turn up to an interview without it?

EFFECTIVE INTERVIEW PREPARATION

1. **Do your research** – Make sure that you've thoroughly researched the company. It's so easy to do now that we have everything at our fingertips. Visit their website and use Google them to find out any current news stories. Not having looked at a company's website is unforgivable. When I interview, I always ask the question, *"What did you think of our website?"* By my reckoning, if someone can't be bothered to look at the company website, then we can't be bothered to look at them!

   You may even consider a couple of questions to ask the recruiter based on what you've seen on their website. A word of caution here if you choose to do this (especially if you're interviewing for an IT or marketing role and you're asked for your opinion about the website layout or content) DON'T CRITICISE THEIR WEBSITE! That's a mistake candidates often make and a sure fire way to talk yourself out of the role. If asked for feedback, make sure it's constructive e.g. *"I like what you did here [ ] and you could expand on that by doing X, Y, Z."* No interviewer will thank you for verbally bashing their website.

2. **For management positions, know the numbers** (especially important for senior management/board roles) – Get hold of the company's accounts from Companies House. It doesn't cost much and will help you prepare more thoroughly. It also looks impressive if you've gone to that much trouble. Also, **know your own numbers** e.g. your current company's turnover, your budget, your KPIs, etc., knowing your numbers is an absolute must. There's nothing more off-putting for a recruiter than a manager who doesn't know his/her figures.

3. **Identify your relevant transferable skills and achievements** – Recruiters want to know what's in it for them if they recruit you. Being clear on your transferable skills and how you would use them for the job is vital. They will also want to hear about your significant achievements in your current/previous roles. If you've done your CV using the format outlined in this book, you'll already have identified them.

4. **Prepare your answers using the STAR format** – Once you have your key achievements, using this format is the easiest way of recalling them at interview is to put them into a format that you can easily remember.

5. **Practise your answers** (role play them) – The more times you practise saying your STAR format answers out loud, the easier it

will be to remember them in an interview. When we say something repeatedly out loud, we build strong neural pathways within the brain which makes it easy to access them in stressful/adverse situations.

TOP TIP

6. **Practise talking through your CV/career history in five minutes** – Whether you're having a CV based interview or a competency based one you need to know your CV and be able to talk it through (without looking at it if possible) for at least five minutes. You'd be amazed how many people can't do that. The more times you practise it, the easier it will become. Don't be caught out with this one; you will ALWAYS get asked about your CV and your career history.

7. **Prepare questions you want to ask** – It never ceased to amaze me how so few people have intelligent questions to ask at the end. Asking quality questions are one of those small things that will make a significant difference to your performance. It may seem like a small thing, but if a recruiter has two excellent candidates who are neck and neck after an interview and one asks a couple of really great questions, to which one do you think the recruiter will offer the role? The type of questions you should ask, and more importantly, those you shouldn't, are covered later in this chapter.

USING THE S.T.A.R. FORMAT

The STAR format is a universally accepted acronym used for structuring answers to interview questions – especially competency based questions. You may be thinking, *"But, how do I know what questions they're going to ask me?"* That's simple; **THEY WILL ASK YOU ABOUT YOUR ACHIEVEMENTS** – interviewing really isn't rocket science.

Hopefully, you're now starting to see the connection between putting your achievements on your CV and your interview preparation. If you've already thought about them and written them down when you did your CV, you're half way there with your interview preparation.

For interview preparation purposes, you're going to take your key achievements and break them down into the STAR format. STAR stands for:

Situation – Set the scene – What was the 'global' or big picture issue i.e. the wider problem that had to be solved. The 'Situation' should account for 10% of your answer.

Task – What needed to be done by you – What was *your* role in solving the global issue? What were you tasked with achieving? What was your goal? The 'Task' accounts for 10% of your answer.

Action – Thinking, saying and doing – What actions did you take to achieve your goal? To whom did you speak? Where did you visit? What research did you do? Did you manage a team? Did you have a budget? Did you use specific project management techniques? List anything that you had to do, think or say to reach the desired result. Your actions should account for 70% of your overall answer as the recruiter will want to see how you demonstrate your key skills and hear about how you achieve your results.

Result – You should clearly define the result with tangible evidence. The more facts and figures that you can add in here the better e.g. money saved/earned, percentages, KPIs, customers gained, customers serviced, business improvements and how the result contributed to the overall success of the organisation. The 'Result' is the section that corresponds with the *'so what'* test I mentioned in the achievements section of your CV. If you can say, *"so what"* after reading the result/outcome, you haven't written enough. The result should form 10% of your overall answer.

The following is a shortened example of the STAR format using my achievement of writing this book. (Note: I haven't written as much as I would if I was preparing for a real interview. My aim here is simply to give you an idea of how to use the STAR structure and what to write under each heading.)

USING THE S.T.A.R. FORMAT

- **Situation** – People looking for a new job don't always know how to go about an effective job search, how to apply for roles or how to successfully manage assessment processes. They also find the whole process, especially going for interviews particularly nerve-wracking and stressful. (*This is the 'global' issue.)*

- **Task** - Based on my years of experience as a recruiter and as a career management coach, I decided to write a book that would provide job hunters with the tools and techniques necessary to help them land the job of their dreams. *(This is my role in delivering a solution to the global issue.)*

- **Action:**

  1. I reviewed the outplacement and redeployment workshops that my company currently provides to our corporate clients. These workshops include CV writing, job hunting,

interview skills, presentation skills, etc.

2. I examined the feedback from workshops to see if there was additional information that I could incorporate into the book.

3. I met with recruitment consultants, in-house recruiters, assessors and HR professionals from my network to clearly understand what recruiters look for during the various assessments and to learn the common mistakes that candidates make.

4. Using my knowledge and the information I gained during my research I wrote the book, which also involved designing the accompanying 'additional resources.'

5. I commissioned the book cover and website design.

6. I edited my text and had the book professionally proofread and edited.

7. I designed and implemented a marketing plan to maximise sales.

(These were some of the actions that I took to achieve the desired result and solve the global issue.)

- **Result** - The book sold over X copies within X months producing revenue of £X to date. As a consequence of the book,

'What Next' has now been commissioned to run career management workshops for new and existing clients with forecast revenue of £X in 2016/17. *(This is what happened as a result of my actions – notice I've included facts and figures).*

Once you have hand-written at least eight achievements in the STAR format, practise reading them out loud so that they become very familiar. As I mentioned earlier, a recruiter is going to test you on your achievements, and if you've done this work up front, ahead of your interview, you're less likely to go 'blank' during the interview itself. The more times you practise reading and reciting your achievements out loud the easier it will be to access them effortlessly during an interview.

WRITING YOUR ACHIEVEMENTS IN THE STAR FORMAT IS THE MOST CRITICAL PART OF YOUR INTERVIEW PREPARATION – IF YOU DECIDE NOT TO DO IT, THEN YOU CAN'T EXPECT TO ACHIEVE EXCEPTIONAL RESULTS.

COMPETENCY BASED INTERVIEWS

You should always use the STAR format to prepare for all interviews, no matter what the type. However, it's particularly important to use this format for competency interview preparation. If you're in doubt about the kind of interview you'll be having, don't be afraid to ask the recruiter, they should be happy to tell you. If it is a competency based interview, you should request a copy of the competencies that you are going to be assessed against. Competencies are sometimes called 'values' or 'behaviours' depending on the company or organisation.

If they don't provide you with a copy, you can usually find them on the organisation's website. Search for 'Company Values', 'Our Values', 'Core Values', 'Behaviours' or 'Competencies' or look for the company's mission statement and you'll usually find them alongside.

WHAT ARE COMPETENCIES/CORE VALUES

Competencies or core values are the guiding principles that define how an organisation behaves. Competencies/core values help companies determine if they are on the right path and fulfilling their business goals; and they create a guide which all employees, clients, and providers should be aware of.

The following is a short list of typical company values/ competencies:

- Honesty
- Respect
- Customer first
- Staff development

- Innovation
- Creativity
- Courageousness
- Commitment

TOP TIP

Once you've written your eight achievements in long-hand, carefully read the company's competencies and assign the most appropriate one for each of your achievements. For example, if I was going for an interview for a company who had the same competencies as I've listed above, I could say my 'book' achievement demonstrated 'Innovation' and 'Creativity.' If I were then asked a question about being creative or innovative, I'd be able to give my 'book' example to demonstrate that competency.

It's possible that you will find that two or three competencies fit any one of your achievements. If that's the case, try not to repeat yourself by using the same example more than once. That's why I suggest that you prepare at least eight achievements. If the company has more than eight competencies (unlikely, but possible), then you'll need to come up with more achievements to illustrate them.

COMPETENCY BASED QUESTIONS

As I've mentioned, competency based questions are designed to test your knowledge, experience, aptitude that match the company's competencies, and you will be scored based on the quality of your answers. When the recruiter is creating the questions, they will make a list of all the parts that make an answer excellent, mediocre or a fail. Depending on your replies, they will assign a score based on how what you say matches against their benchmark.

Typical competency based questions start with:

- *"Give me an example of a time when you've had to..."*
- *'"Tell me when you've delivered..."*
- *"When did you last have experience of...?"*

Going back to my 'book' example and the competency of creativity, I may be asked, *"Give me an example of when you have done something creative (or innovative) that has added value."* I would then give them my answer using the STAR format I'd prepared.

ANSWERING INTERVIEW QUESTIONS

TOP TIP

It's fine to respond to questions making reference to the STAR format, for example:

- *"The situation was..."*

- *"My task was…"*
- *"The action I took was…"*
- *"The results were…"*

No good interviewer will have a problem with you doing that. It's also an excellent way to stay on track if you know that you occasionally wander and get a bit lost when answering questions. It's relatively common for interviewees to forget the question half way through their answer. Using the STAR format will help to keep you on track.

TOP TIP

Once you have your eight achievements written in long-hand, you then need to shorten them to bullet points using a few key words as prompts. For example, again using my 'book' example, I would write:

- **Situation** - People not confident at job hunting.
- **Task** - wrote a book to help address issues.
- **Actions** - Researched, wrote, published and marketed book.
- **Result** - Sold x copies, delivered x programmes, outcome £x revenue.

Once you've done this exercise for all eight of your achievements, either transcribe them onto small cards or A4 sheets with two achievements per page, writing the corresponding competency at the top of each achievement. You can then take these into the interview with you, just in case you 'go blank' when asked a question. Any notes you take in with you should only be used as a prompt. They are *your* achievements, after all, so you shouldn't have to read them verbatim.

I strongly urge you to take your STAR format bullet notes into interviews, especially if you know that you get nervous or have a have a tendency to go 'blank.' The majority of clients find that they never need to refer to their notes, but just knowing that they have them to fall back on, if necessary, is a big comfort.

TAKING NOTES TO INTERVIEWS

1. **If you do need to refer to your notes, ask the interviewer first** – Say something like, *"I haven't had an interview for a while, and so I took the initiative and wrote some notes to bring with me. Do you mind if I refer to them?"* Very few interviewers will say no, and if they do, you have to ask yourself if that's the kind of company for whom you want to work. Don't ask at the beginning of the interview as it sets the wrong tone; only ask when/if you need to.

   If a candidate does ask to look at their notes, it tells the recruiter that they know where their weaknesses are, and they have taken steps to address them. All the recruiters/assessors I've spoken to about this topic, totally agree on this.

2. **Make sure you space your notes out** – Type them using a large font or use neat large block handwriting that can be read without difficulty when you're under pressure.

3. **Don't take in your long hand notes with you** - You will never be able to read them in a pressurised environment, and it will have the opposite effect than what you would hope; making your more feel flustered and out of control.

With all the clients I've personally coached through the career management process, I can only recall two needing to use their notes. The first completely ignored my advice to only take in bullet point notes and proceeded to tie himself up in knots as he tried desperately to read his long-hand achievements. He didn't get the job.

The second hadn't had an interview for approximately 30 years and happened to lose his way during an answer. He asked the interviewer if he could review his notes, which he did briefly with their consent, enabling him to get quickly right back on track. The feedback from the interviewer was they were impressed with his preparation which contributed toward their decision to offer him the role.

PREPARING USING THE S.T.A.R. FORMAT AND COMPANY COMPETENCIES

1. You should have at least eight achievements preferably from the last three years, which you should prepare using the STAR format.

2. You should write at least a page of A4 for each achievement or as near to that as you can get to it.

3. Handwrite your STAR achievements. I know it's a pain as we're so used to typing everything now; however, we make a strong connection in our brains when we physically write something down, making it easier to recall during an interview.

4. Once you've written your achievements in long-hand, you need to carefully read the company's competencies and assign the most relevant one to each of your achievements.

5. Distill each of your key achievements into key bullet points and put them on either individual cards or two per A4 sheet, carefully spaced out with the competency at the top of each and take them with you into the interview.

6. If you've been part of or managed a large project containing different elements, it's likely that you'll be able to split it down into more than one achievement demonstrating different competencies.

7. Even if you don't have a competency interview, using the START format is still an excellent way to prepare (although obviously it's unlikely that you'll have competencies to assign to your achievements). You should use the STAR format to plan for the following types of meetings/interviews:

    - Meetings with recruitment consultants
    - Telephone interviews
    - Face to face interviews
    - Video interviews
    - Skype/Bluejeans interviews

TOP TEN MOST FREQUENTLY ASKED QUESTIONS

As well as competency based questions, there are also frequently asked questions for which you should prepare answers. They don't need to be in the STAR format; however, you should give them some thought and jot down ideas of how you would answer them.

TOP TIP

Every single client that my colleagues and I have worked with in a career management capacity has been asked at least two of these questions at *every* interview (N.B you *don't* need to write your answers to these questions in the STAR format):

1. ***"Tell me about yourself/Talk me through your CV"*** – The interviewer is saying *"I want to hear you talk."* These are common questions to get the interview started and put you at ease. Be able to talk through your CV, your personal attributes and qualifications in around five minutes, emphasising the experience and skills that are relevant to the job.

2. ***"What are your strengths?"*** – The interviewer wants a straightforward answer as to what you are good at and how you're going to add value. Your strengths lie in the skills you have that will separate you from other candidates, so list three or four and explain how they could benefit the employer. Strengths to consider include technical proficiency, determination to succeed, positive attitude, ability to learn quickly, the capacity to relate to people and achieve a common goal. You may be asked to give examples of the above so be prepared.

3. *"What are your weaknesses/development areas?"*– The interviewer is asking about your self-perception and self-awareness. **DON'T GIVE THEM A REASON NOT TO EMPLOY YOU!** Asking about your weaknesses or development areas is another standard question for which you can be well prepared. **It's not appropriate to say that you don't have any** as everyone has growth areas; no matter how good they are at their job.

You have two options when answering this type of question. The first is to use a weakness such as a lack of experience (not ability) in an area that is not vital for the job, and tell them how you would go about addressing it.

The second option is to describe a weakness that could also be considered as a strength and the steps you would take to combat it. An example would be, *"Attention to detail is important to me, and I can't afford information to go out from my team that isn't correct as it could cost the company thousands of pounds. I realised that I was becoming a bottleneck because I wanted to check everything personally, which was starting to affect deadlines. I, therefore, put a new process in place where my team checks each other's work before it goes out. That way I'm no longer a bottleneck, and we are continuing to hit our deadlines."*

Do not select a personal weakness such as *"I'm not a morning person. However, I'm much better as the day goes on"* That's a real example of how a candidate answered this question, again, don't give the recruiter a reason not to employ you.

4. ***"What's the biggest mistake you've made and how did you correct it?"*** - The interviewer is trying to find out what your definition of a mistake is and whether you show a logical approach to problem-solving using your initiative. Give them an example of something small. Describe how you defined the problem, what the options were, why you selected the one you did and what the outcome was. Always end on a positive note. N.B. They may also ask what you would do differently next time.

5. ***"How do you like to be managed?"*** - The interviewer wants to find out whether you can work on your own initiative or whether you need close supervision. The perfect way to answer this question is, *"I like to be left to get on with my job but know that there's support there if I need it."* This statement will give the recruiter confidence that you're not high maintenance and get things done without having to be told.

6. ***"How would your colleagues or manager describe you?"*** – It never ceases to amaze me how people are still surprised

when they get asked this question, as it's fairly standard. The correct answer would be, *"I think that they would describe me as trustworthy, honest and supportive and a team player"* or *"honest, hardworking, conscientious"* etc. Again, reflect on the type of person the recruiter is looking for, and then choose which adjectives that best describe you. Remember to check the company's competencies or person specification, if they are available, and tailor your answer to them.

7. ***"What don't you like about your current job?"*** – Be careful how you respond to this one. There are always aspects of our jobs that we dislike; so it's not appropriate to say *"nothing."* Choose something small and inconsequential or something that you don't like doing, but you've found a way to make it enjoyable or even fun.

8. ***"What's the reason for leaving your current employer?"*** – The interviewer is trying to understand and evaluate your motives for moving. If you're leaving of your own accord, state that you're looking for a new challenge, more responsibility, the opportunity to gain additional experience or a change of environment, etc. Avoid being negative and never cite 'salary' as the primary motivator.

    If you have been made redundant, say so. It's no reflection on you or how you did your job, so don't try to cover it up. Be open and explain the company's reasons for the restructure, remember that it was your *job* that was made redundant, not you.

9. ***"Why do you want to work here?"*** - The interviewer wants to find out just how much you know about the company and the role. They want evidence that the job suits you, fits in with your general aptitudes, coincides with your long-term goals and involves things you enjoy doing. Make sure you have a good understanding of the role and the organisation and describe what is attracting you to the role/company. Use information from the company's website to get a good feel for their culture, products, services, social responsibility, etc.

10. ***"Why should we give the job to you?"*** – I ask this question at every interview without fail. Why? Because if you don't know why a company should recruit you, then how would they know? It's a question that many native Britons find difficult to answer, that's because we are typically brought up not to brag about our achievements, resulting in us feeling uncomfortable when forced to tell a prospective employer how good we are. The problem with that is if you don't tell them, the next person will. Your answer to this question could mean the difference between landing the job or not.

A good reply to this would be, *"You should recruit me because I think I'm an excellent fit with your company and the role, not just because of my skills and experience, but because of culture and values too. I know I can do a brilliant job for you, and I'd relish the opportunity to make a difference."* Sounds a bit cheesy, but it's what a recruiter wants to hear.

Managers may also get asked:

11. ***"How do you like to manage?"*** - The interviewer wants to find out whether you like to control everything around you or whether you're more easy-going. A good way to answer this question is, *"I like to leave my staff to get on with their jobs, but know that I'm here to support them if they need me."* Followed by, *"I like to set clear goals with achievable timescales so that my team knows what I expect of them. I regularly check in with them to see that they are managing their workload and deadlines effectively"*.

12. ***"What do you think your priorities will be in the first three months?"*** – Here, the interviewer is looking to see if you've grasped the main elements of the role as well as the potential problems. They are interested in hearing how you will evaluate, plan and organise your time including, how you would get to know the business, understand the challenges and start to plan for the future.

13. *"How do you manage stress"* – Most management roles are stressful. Therefore, the recruiter will want to know what you do to relieve stress and how you handle stressful situations. If you get asked this question, they will be looking for two things, utilisation of your skills (organising, planning, delegating, etc.) as well as what you physically do outside work to manage stress (exercise, holidays, hobbies, etc.).

HOBBIES AND INTERESTS

It's likely that the recruiter will ask you about your hobbies and interests. Be careful with this one and give it some thought before the interview. As I discussed in the 'Additional Information' section in Chapter 3, companies like it when candidates have hobbies and interests that align with their values. Make sure you have something interesting to talk about, and it should be current, not something you've done in the dim and distant past.

I recently heard of a candidate who went for an interview with a forward thinking company who only recruit people with drive, ambition and who want to make a difference. She had done a fantastic interview and ticked all the boxes with her answers, only to completely blow her chances at the last hurdle. As she was being escorted out of the building, the recruiter asked her what she was doing over the weekend. Without thinking, she replied, *"I'm having a complete chill out this weekend, you know, onesie and a full on Netflix binge."*

Up until that point, the recruiter was planning to offer her the role. However, her weekend plans were the complete opposite of what he would expect from the type of person that would fit with the organisation and that was enough of a reason for him to to reject her.

YOUR QUESTIONS FOR THE INTERVIEWER

The questions you ask at an interview are much more important than most candidates think. They may seem like such a small part of the process, however, if you're in direct competition with another candidate and there's little to differentiate between the two of you, the questions you ask can make all the difference.

Your chance to ask the recruiter questions tends to be at the end of the interview and unfortunately, by this point, most candidates are a bit tired, a little 'wrung out' and just want to get out of there. Therefore, for many candidates there can be a temptation to say, *"No thank you. You've answered everything as we've gone along."* I'm always disappointed when I get this response; it's simply not acceptable.

TOP TIP

Make a list of around ten, quality questions and take them to the interview with you. That's not to say that you'll ask all ten, you will probably be given time to pose around two or three. Preparing more will give you options in case some get answered during the interview.

Your questions should be in extra large print and well spaced out on a sheet of A4 paper so that you can read them easily when you're under pressure. We can find it difficult to read small type print with tight line spacing when we're stressed. When the interviewer asks if you have any questions, you can produce the sheet from your nicely presented folder and ask anything important, that's still outstanding.

Planning your questions beforehand not only shows the interviewer that you prepare, but it ensures that you ask quality questions rather than searching around for something on the spare of the moment, or even worse, not having anything to ask.

Interviews are a two-way process – you need to be sure that the job is right for you, every bit as much as the company knowing you're right for them. Asking quality questions is your chance to interview the company, obtaining answers that you need to enable you to make the right decision if they offer you the role.

Here are some generic questions that usually work well:

- ***"How could I impress you in my first three months?"*** - The answer to this will tell you how they would like to see you perform and the areas where you should be concentrating if you were successful. It also shows the recruiter that you're thinking ahead and want to do what's best for the company as well as for yourself.

- ***"What challenges could I face in the first three months?"*** - It's worth being aware of any challenges that may stop you reaching your objectives. The fact that you're asking about them at the interview shows that you're aware of that possibility and want to work through or around them to succeed.

- ***"Is there anything you would like to improve in your department and how could I help?"*** – Asking this shows that you're clearly keen to be part of the team from day one and contribute to the broader goals of the department and the wider company.

- ***"What's the working environment like?"* or *"How would you describe the company's culture?"*** – If the interviewer hasn't covered this area during the interview, ask about it. It'll help you understand if you would fit in. Make sure what they tell you fits in with your expectations and your requirements.

- *"Will I receive any development in the role?"* – It's important to find out what sort of opportunities there are for promotion in future (if that's important to you) and to ask it without coming across as if you want to leap into a more senior job before you've got the first one. It also shows the interviewer you're committed to learning and growing within the company.

Here are some other excellent questions to ask:

- *"How/why has the position become available?"*
- *"Can you describe my area of responsibility?"*
- *"How does the role/department fit into the structure of the organisation as a whole?"*
- *"Who will I be reporting to?"*
- *"How would you describe your company's culture?"*
- *"How will my performance be evaluated?"*
- *"Is there a clearly defined career path?"*
- *"What would I be expected to do on a typical day?"*
- *"What do you like about working here?"* (I really like that question, as it turns the emphasis back on the recruiter and will make them think.)

Of course, you may have some questions of your own from your research around the job content or organisation. You should ask questions that are important to you, and that will help you make the right choice if you're offered the role.

At the end of the interview, you should remember to ask:

- ***"What are the next stages and when can I expect to hear about the outcome?"*** – It can sometimes take a while for hiring managers to come to a decision, and that can be frustrating. Hearing about whether you've got a job or not may be *everything* to you. However, it's only one of many tasks for the recruiter. Try to find out potential dates for further interviews/assessment centres or some indication that they want to take your application further.

You shouldn't use this question in place of any of the ones mentioned earlier. Despite what many candidates think and some career advisers suggest, it doesn't say anything positive about you and your thought processes – it is a secondary question. Therefore, while it is important to ask, it should be left until the very end of the interview.

QUESTIONS NOT TO ASK

Of course, there are also some questions that you should *never* ask, these include:

- **Anything to do with pay (especially sick pay!)** – Towards the beginning of my HR career, I interviewed hundreds if not thousands of candidates for Warehouse Operative positions. I remember one candidate asking about the company's sick pay scheme. What that screams to a recruiter is: *"I INTEND TO BE OFF SICK ... A LOT! HOW MUCH WILL I GET PAID?"*
- *"What days/hours will I be working?"*
- *"Will I have to work weekends?"*
- *"Is there a bonus scheme?"*
- *"Can I work from home?"*
- *"What does your company do?"*
- *"What's this job for again?"*
- *"When can I take time off for a holiday?"*
- *"How long would I have to wait to get promoted?"*
- *"How long is the lunch break?"*
- *"Does this company monitor Internet usage?"*
- *"How many warnings do you get before you get sacked?"*
- *"Did I get the job?"*

(All the questions above are real life examples of questions that candidates have asked interview.)

I realise it may be important for you to know the answer to some of these questions. However, you should find them out **BEFORE** the meeting (unless that is, that you know the interviewer is going to talk about them in the interview). We all know that we go to work for money, and it's important to have a good work/life balance. However, if you ask anything about money/hours, etc. the recruiter will think that's all you're bothered about, which may well be true; however, you shouldn't let them know that. Every company likes to think that you want to work for them because they're such a fabulous employer, and that's what you should leave them believing.

It's much better to negotiate the salary, benefits, hours, etc. when you get offered the role. You're in a much stronger position then because the employer is 'bought in' to you. They've also potentially spent a lot of money getting to the offer stage and therefore, at this point you'll find it's much easier to negotiate the package you want. There's more information regarding Job Offers in Chapter 8.

SECOND INTERVIEWS

You will have done the majority of the preparation needed for a second interview when you prepared for the first. While your second interview may be with a different interviewer, you can't leave that to chance. Even if they are different interviewers, it's likely that they'll have a copy of the initial interview notes, especially if it was a competency based interview. Therefore, expect some repetition from the first, but try to keep answers fresh.

SECOND INTERVIEW PREPARATION

1. **Review your performance in the first interview** – Be self-critical about what went well and what needs to improve. Work on anything you think needs to be adjusted.

2. **Identify any material you didn't cover** – Make a note of any preparation that you didn't use at the first interview. Rather than repeating yourself, it's always good to introduce new information, examples, and achievements at second interview.

3. **Find out the type of interview you'll be having –** Ask whether you will have a competency or CV based interview.

4. **Prepare new examples for competency based interviews** – If you used all your achievements in the first interview, write some new ones (you may want to consider using ones from a previous role, preferably where the role was within the last three years).

5. **Carry out more research** – Review what you were told about the company in the first interview. Is there any more research you can do based on what you learnt? Do you know anyone who works there? If so, try and speak to them to get an insider view on culture, current 'hot topics,' buzz words and the types of questions to ask that will impress.

6. **Prepare your questions for them** – Ask any questions that didn't get answered in the first interview, but also include any that you may have on reflection.

ASSESSMENT CENTRES

It's increasingly common for companies to use assessment centres for management, senior management, graduate and professional roles (e.g. IT, Sales, HR, and Marketing). Many organisations consider selection centres to be the best way to test a candidate's all round skills, knowledge, experience including their interpersonal skills. Assessment centres can last anything from a couple of hours to a couple of days.

Large corporations and public sector organisations, including many charities, councils, and NHS tend to use assessment centres for most of their vacancies no matter what the level or role. They view Assessment Centres as the most reliable way to recruit quality employees.

Assessment Centres work by having a selection of exercises or tasks which are scored in much the same way as competency based interviews. The candidate with the highest overall score at the end of the assessment is usually the one who is offered the job, provided that they hit the benchmark figure. As discussed when we covered competency based interviews, assessment centres are designed to find the right overall person for the role, and to avoid 'face fits' syndrome or any potential claims of discrimination.

For management, professional or graduate positions, candidates will often be provided with information based on a fictitious, but similar company. This information can include documentation relating to an overview of the company, performance data, customer satisfaction surveys, etc. The assessors will base the assessment centre's exercises on that information. Using a fictitious company is the closest way a recruiter has of understanding how you would deal with similar situations, tasks, and interactions in a real life scenario. However, this isn't always the case. Some companies base their assessments loosely on similar everyday activities within their own organisation.

TOP TIP

An assessment centre is designed to test candidates on the company's competencies as well as their skills, experience and aptitude for the role. Therefore, it's important to ensure that you have a copy of competencies before the assessment centre so that you can familiarise yourself with the criteria you will be assessed against, and identify where your skills and experience match.

OVERNIGHT STAYS/DINNER/DRINKS

Where an assessment centre is over two days, there will usually be a dinner and drinks involved. Spending social time with the candidates is not merely something arranged for practical reasons; it is an integral part of the selection process. In a social setting, the assessors get to see first-hand how candidates interact with others on a personal level. Often, senior managers/directors who are not involved directly in the assessments are invited to evening activities so that they can meet the candidates and better assess their personality 'fit' for the organisation. It also enables candidates to ask questions of the people who run the company providing them with the opportunity to learn more about the culture first-hand.

ASSESSMENT CENTRE DINNERS/DRINKS

1. **DON'T GET DRUNK!** – If you drink, having a couple is fine, that's being sociable. However, getting drunk is totally unacceptable. Unfortunately, I've witnessed candidates having too much to drink, either causing a scene or making a fool of themselves, only to have to face the assessment team and the other candidates the next morning. Make no mistake; the dinner/drinks are every bit as much a part of the selection process as the formal exercises. If you fail this test, you will, without a doubt, fail the whole assessment – no matter how well you do with everything else.

2. **Keep your views about the other candidates or the assessors to yourself** – Don't ever get drawn into gossiping about other candidates or the assessors. You never know who may overhear or who may relay your views to the assessors (it is a competition after all!).

3. **Don't 'suck up' to the assessors/management team** – Be polite and engaging, ask questions and show interest. However, don't try and monopolise a person's time. It will annoy them and is likely to have the opposite effect to what you were hoping to achieve. There have been times when managers have said to me, *"Please save me from this girl/guy, they're so full on, I can't get away from them!"* You don't want to be remembered for the wrong reason.

4. **Take note of the dress code** – Usually, the dress code for dinner/drinks is smart/casual. That means no trainers, t-shirts, vests, sportswear. Men should wear, dark, clean jeans/chinos (no light, faded or ripped jeans), dark trousers are fine with an open necked shirt and a jacket. Ladies, please ensure that you don't dress provocatively with too much skin on show. A smart dress or dark jeans/skirt/ trousers with a neat blouse/shirt are acceptable.

   If in doubt, ask about the dress code and examples of what they mean. I always prefer people to ask rather than turn up unprepared. Remember they are assessing how you present yourself in a more casual environment and whether you still remain professional. This gives the recruiter a good indication of how you would behave if you were representing the company externally.

5. **Prepare something interesting to say** – If you know that you're uncomfortable in social situations, plan some topics to talk around and casually drop them into the conversation as and when you think it's appropriate.

6. **Use the opportunity to network** – If you do feel a bit uncomfortable, you may have a tendency not to circulate, preferring instead to stay with one or two people with whom you feel at ease. However, that won't help you in this scenario. Make sure that you work your way around the room and talk to as many people as possible. If you don't speak to a representative of the company, they will notice or even worse; they won't see you at all. Building relationships with the right people, but without monopolising their time, is important.

ASSESSMENT CENTRE CONTENT

Here's a list of the most typical assessment centre activities:

1. **Group task** – The group task is performed with other candidates and is a good way to get a feel for your competition. When it comes to group tasks, it's a common

misapprehension that the most vocal, pushy person, who immediately takes the lead, forcing their opinion on others, will score the most points. This couldn't be further from the truth. The assessors will mark you on your contribution to the group's overall task achievement and how you demonstrate your skills that match the company's competencies for example:

- **Listening skills** – They want to know if you can listen to instructions, it is an essential part of any exercise. I've seen many group tasks fail because candidates don't listen carefully to the requirements of the activity. The assessors will also want to see whether you listen to your colleagues and if you take their views/suggestions into account.

- **How you work with and relate to others** – They will be looking to see if you can collaborate with a team but also how you lead if that's a skill required in the role. They will want to know if you're supportive of your teammates.

- **The balance between your contribution and valuing others** – They will test whether you can get your point across without bullying or forcing your opinion and encourage others' ideas.

- **Being assertive but not overbearing** – It's important to show your leadership skills. However, being a leader does not mean ignoring others' opinions and asserting your own.

- **Inviting quieter members to join in** – This is of crucial importance. Good leaders will invite quieter people to join in because they are usually the 'thinkers' of the group, the ones that tend to consider everything before jumping in head first. They can be invaluable in a team effort as they usually take into consideration the issue as a whole and see problems that others may not.

- **Don't volunteer to be the scribe/note taker -** Most people think that they look proactive if they nominate themselves to take the group's notes. However, the scribe is usually too busy writing to be able to take a fully active part in completing the task – **if you don't participate actively, you will receive fewer marks**.

If you do decide to scribe, don't use a flip chart; write from a position within the group. Once you remove yourself from the group, (which you automatically do when standing up) you'll be less involved and unlikely to be included critical decisions, making it almost impossible to receive a good score.

- **Avoid performing the role of facilitator** – Again, it's difficult for the assessors to mark you when you're facilitating and not taking an active part in tasks.

- TOP TIP **KEEP FOCUS ON THE TIME** – Especially if you nominate yourself or get appointed as the timekeeper. Another reason most group tasks fail is because of a lack of time management, even when there is a timekeeper. Often, team members get so involved with solving the problem that they forget about the time altogether. Everyone in your team will lose points if you go over time and don't manage to complete the task.

2. **Presentation** – During presentations you are being tested not just your technical ability, but how you prepare, work under pressure, your communication skills and if you're able to speak publically with confidence. I cover presentations in detail in Chapter 8.

3. **Competency/Panel Interview** – Companies use competency based interviews to test your experience, achievements, and skills. All delegates are asked the same questions based on the company's competencies. The assessors mark each answer against criteria decided during the design stage.

4. **Psychometric/Personality Testing** – These tests are designed to assess your softer, interpersonal skills and behaviours. Often a company will require you to complete such a test before the assessment centre as part of their pre-selection process; however, some do still use them on the day.

   These are online tests with approximately 100 questions which will be in a multiple choice or an 'either/or' format. You may find that the same questions are repeated throughout the test, although they may be phrased slightly differently. The different phrasing is intentional, designed to check that you are answering questions truthfully, rather than in the way you *think* you should. These tests are so sophisticated that they will highlight any anomalies in your responses, and generate a score that indicates how truthful you've been.

   Once completed, a report will automatically be produced showing your strengths and potential development areas. It will also provide the recruiter with a range of questions to ask designed to probe your weaker areas. Unfortunately, there's little preparation you can do for this as they focus on your personality and how you typically behave. However, there are various websites where you can practise taking these types of tests for free.

Make sure that you answer **honestly** using your first thoughts and your gut feeling. The more you think about a question, usually the harder it will be to answer. There's no right or wrong here, you are who you are, so answer truthfully.

5. **Verbal/Numerical/Technical/Mechanical Testing** – These tests assess your aptitude for Maths and English as well as your technical abilities required for the role. Again you will complete them online. See 'Online Testing' earlier in this chapter for more information.

6. **In-Tray Exercise** – There are many examples of in-tray exercises. In essence, they consist of a piece of work which deliberately relates to something you would be required to do in the role. For example, for an accountant, it could be data analysis, for a PA it could be to write a formal letter, for a sales person it could be to devise a sample sales plan.

There's little preparation you can do for in-tray exercises. Remember to read the instructions carefully and stick to time. Avoid trying to plan everything in rough (although an outline is fine) as you may run out of time.

7. **Role Play** – Role play is similar to an in-tray exercise in that it will base based on something that could happen in a day-to-day situation. For example, if the role entails managing difficult people (customers or staff), you may be given a scenario where you have to work through a problem with an actor or member of the assessment team playing the part of a tricky employee/customer. You will usually be given the situation beforehand with time to prepare. Don't be surprised if it's filmed as it's standard practice. It also provides a record in case a candidate challenges their score at a later date.

With role play the assessor will want to see:

- How you handle difficult situations
- How you build relationships and rapport with others
- Whether you take responsibility for what's happening
- Your problem solving and interpersonal skills
- How you prepare (if you're given the scenario before the actual role play)
- How you work/behave under pressure

TOP TIP

Consider the ***outcome*** you want to achieve – this is paramount and where most people fall down. Think about the result you want and write down some key questions/areas that you need to explore in order to get to your desired outcome. If the role play involves an awkward person, one of your questions should be, *"What would you like the outcome to be?"*, then you can explore together where there may be synergies/areas for compromise between your desired outcome and theirs.

8. **Written Reports** – Written reports are usually designed based on a case study intended to test your comprehension, analytical and problem-solving skills. They also give an indication of how good your written English is, as well as your ability to follow instructions. Make sure you stick to time and write a quick outline covering the key items you want to include. Spend as little time as possible on the outline and start writing your end document as soon as possible. Remember not to waffle, but be concise and succinct. The following is a standard report outline:

    a. Introduction
    b. Main Body
    c. Summary/Conclusion/Recommendations.

Alternatively, try thinking outside the box and present the information in a different way. Unless expressly stated, you don't have to write a full report, consider how you might display the information pictorially in a table or graph for example. Presenting information in an alternative format while still answering the question will automatically help you stand out from your competitors.

Put yourself in the assessor's shoes and think about how you'd like to see the information presented. The feedback I have from assessors is that they get tired of reading and marking hundreds of reports that are full of waffle! They give a sigh of relief when someone presents the right information in an alternative way. *Remember to keep an eye on the time.*

9. **Self-Review** – A self-review is a written report that is usually completed at the end of an assessment centre. You'll be asked to evaluate your performance, describe what went well, what you could have done better/differently and what you've learnt. Remember that they are looking for people who can demonstrate the company's competencies, so bear that in mind when you complete your review. They will also want to know how self-aware you are, whether you notice your mistakes and how you would handle the same

problem if it came up again. They will also want to know if you have recognised any development areas.

Unfortunately, again, there's little preparation you can do for this. However, don't be over critical of yourself, be honest giving reasons (where possible) for your actions, together with plans to address development areas.

10. **Meeting with a Manager** – This is different to the competency based interview. It's often positioned at the end of the day providing you with the opportunity to give and receive feedback on the day and to ask any outstanding questions. Again, the manager will be looking for how self-aware you are and if you've picked up on any development areas. You don't usually receive a mark for this part of the assessment.

The following is a list of top tips and common mistakes made by candidates during assessment centres. This information has been collated from the feedback I've received from both assessors and candidates:

ASSESSMENT CENTRES

1. **Don't just do it, show the assessors you're doing it** – If the assessor doesn't see/hear you doing or saying something, they

can't mark it.

2. **Manage your time** – THE top reason people fail during assessment centres is not keeping within the time guidelines stipulated. If you get invited to an assessment centre and you don't have a watch (many people now use their phone to tell the time), either borrow one or buy one, it's an investment worth making. You shouldn't rely on your phone for the time as it's unlikely that you'll be allowed to take it into the assessment with you.

3. **Tackle all sections** – No matter what the task, try to complete all of it. If you miss something out, you could lose valuable marks. In an assessment situation, one point can mean the difference between getting the job and not.

4. **Follow the instructions** – Read and follow the instructions carefully. Don't skim read documents as that could mean that you miss important information.

5. **Don't get sidetracked** – Remember to stay on track and keep reviewing the question/task at hand so that you don't get side tracked. If you don't answer the right question or do something that's not on the agenda, you won't get a score for it, and you'll have wasted valuable time and marks.

6. **Don't plan everything in rough** – This is especially pertinent

when it comes to 'on the day' presentations where you are given the topic and limited time to prepare. You rarely have time to plan everything in rough *and* to re-do it perfectly.

7. **Don't offer to facilitate, be the timekeeper, or scribe** – It's unlikely that you'll be fully involved in tasks if you volunteer to take on these responsibilities, potentially handing valuable points to your competitors.

8. **Practise, practise, practise** – I'll keep saying this repeatedly; practise is massively important. Practise your interview questions, presentations, on-line tests, etc. as many times as possible.

9. **Make sure that you know the competencies** – You should ensure that you thoroughly understand the company's competencies, and can demonstrate them.

10. **Visualise things going well** – By consistently imagining the day from beginning to end, focussing on your desired outcome in as much detail as possible, will greatly increase your chances of achieving that result.

11. **Don't panic!** If you didn't do particularly well in one exercise, try to not let it affect the rest of your performance. It's your *overall* score that counts.

PRESENTATION SKILLS

"Proper preparation prevents presentation predicaments!"

I could write a whole book based purely on presentation skills as it's such a big topic. I run two-day presentation skills workshops, covering not only how to design and deliver an effective presentation but how to understand the psychology of the audience which enables delegates to deliver their message with impact. While I don't have space go into that amount of detail here, I will give you a good solid structure and some top tips which will allow you to prepare and deliver an excellent interview presentation.

Many companies use presentations as a part of their selection process for a range of different jobs. As well as being an integral part of many assessment centres, they are probably the most used assessment tool, after the interview.

WHEN YOU'RE GIVEN THE TITLE ON THE DAY

If you're required to give a presentation, you will usually be provided with the topic/title, the timing (duration) and who your audience will be, before the assessment/interview. However, that's not always the case; some companies prefer to give you the information on the day. If this happens, again, it's important to think about the competencies you will be tested against and have them with you in your folder. Keep calm and quickly draw up an outline of what you want to cover (don't write down too much information in draft, as you could run out of time). Think about the key messages that you want to deliver and shape your content as explained in the six step structure outlined in this chapter (I suggest that you take a copy of this structure with you to refer to).

TOP TIP

The most frequently used presentation titles are based on what you expect to achieve in your first 30/60 or 90 days in the role. Therefore, if you know that you're going to do a presentation on the day, but don't know the title, give some consideration to how you would answer that question. What would you want to learn, deliver and achieve in the first few months in the role? There are some excellent books available regarding 'first 90 days'; it would be worth investing in a couple.

WHAT MAKES A POOR PRESENTATION

There are typical mistakes that people make when preparing and delivering a presentation:

1. Having no clear aim.
2. Not understanding the topic/what information the assessor wants to see/hear.
3. Including information that isn't relevant/ important.
4. Not understanding the audience.

5. Using poor visual aids (we've all heard the term or been witness to 'Death by PowerPoint.'
6. Not sticking to time limits.
7. Being dull and uninteresting.
8. Delivering poorly which is usually a result of inadequate preparation or nerves.
9. Lack of preparation.

PRESENTATION TIMINGS

I have designed an easy to use six step structure that will help you overcome the common presentation mistakes. But before I tell you about that, it's important to look at how to accurately time your presentation and how much information you should include in each section (*what* to include is covered later).

Taking an example of a ten-minute presentation, here's how you should break it down:

TEN MINUTE PRESENTATION		
Opening *(Two minutes)*	**Content** *(Six minutes - two minutes per key point)*	**Ending** *(Two minutes)*
Tell them what you're going to tell them.	Tell them. *(No more than three key points)*	Tell them what you've told them.

If you have more than ten minutes, either add additional key points or explain each key point in more detail. However, I would recommend having a maximum of five points, any more and it will be information overload for your audience and for you!

SIX STEP STRUCTURE

1. **Have a clear aim**

   Make sure you think about and have clear answers to the following questions before you start your preparation:

- Why are you making the presentation?
- What is the purpose?
  - To inform?
  - To persuade/sell?
  - To entertain?
- **What do you want to achieve/what is your desired outcome?** Be clear about your end position. Be SPECIFIC – if you're confused, your audience will be too. What do you want your audience to:
  - Know?
  - Take away?
  - Do differently as a result?
- What knockout result do you want?

2. **Know your audience**

Your audience will be thinking (albeit subconsciously) the following:

- *"Please tell me something I don't already know."*
- *"Please don't waste my time."*
- *"Please give me something that makes my life easier."*

An audience is only interested in the part of your presentation that makes their lives easier; therefore, it's important to be **relevant, concise and compelling. They will also remember what you want them to remember.** The success of your presentation depends on how much what you say coincides with what they want and need to hear.

Consider the following:

- What interests them about the subject?
- What do they already know about the subject?
- What is their 'stake' in the subject?
- What 'baggage' might they have about the subject?
- What issues may be important to them?
- What points may be contentious? (You should avoid being deliberately provocative in an interview situation – you can't afford to have an interviewer turn against you!).

In summary:

- What do you want to persuade your audience to do?
- Decide on the result you're want to achieve.
- Research your audience:
    - Who are they?
    - What do they *want* to hear?
    - What do they *need* to hear?
    - What must you tell them to get what YOU want from giving the presentation?
    - What are the audiences starting positions?

3. **Select the right content**

Create a 'statement' that reflects the essence of your presentation which is short, relevant and memorable. *Everything* in your presentation must relate back to this if it doesn't, ditch it. Your statement should encompass:

- What you want the audience to remember above all else
- What you would say if you only had 10 seconds

Your statement must:

- Be created specifically for that audience.
- Feel crucial to that audience
- Stimulate audience thought
- Be one sentence long

- Be simple enough to be memorable
- Should not just state the end position

Once you have your statement, brainstorm your ideas. There's a great piece of free software that I use for brainstorming and planning content of presentations, workshops and book content. It's useful if you're a visual person and like to see things written down, especially pictorially. The software is called 'Xmind7' (www.xmind.net/).

Brainstorming your ideas:

- Use your 'statement' to brainstorm all the content you could include in your presentation.
- Think about every bit of information available to support your statement e.g. statistics, anecdotes, stories, facts, testimonials, etc., and list the headings.
- Be inclusive rather than exclusive at this stage – leave the editing until later, just get the ideas down for now.
- Group headings together where applicable.

Once you've brainstormed, filter the information using the following criteria:

- **Must know** – The key points that you want to make and the essential information that supports and illustrates them.
- **Should know** – Desirable information that will help the audience understand the bigger picture. You shouldn't include this in the presentation, but could cover it during a Question and Answer session at the end. You may also wish to put this information in handouts.
- **Could know** - Leave this information out, it's not necessary and will take away from the essential message.

In summary:

- Write down, in one sentence, what you want the audience to remember – your statement.
- Brainstorm the information that could flow from the statement.
- Select only the 'must knows' from your brainstorm.
- Put 'should know' information in a handout.
- Leave out the 'could know'.

4. **Shape the content**

Your presentation should have three distinct sections:

a. **Introduction** – *'Tell them what you're going to tell them.'*

- Open with an attention grabber, which includes your 'statement'. The first few seconds are key, open with:
    - A quote or anecdote
    - A relevant startling statistic
    - A promise
    - A rhetorical question
- Your first sentence should be striking enough to make your audience listen – your STATEMENT.
- Be risky rather than bland.
- Give the audience a jolt, but don't turn them off.
- NEVER start with an apology.
- Tell the audience the purpose of the talk.
- Provide the audience with your presentation plan i.e. a preview of the key points you intend covering.

b. **Main body** - *'Tell them.'*

- Have no more than three to five key points – if your presentation is ten minutes, then you should use no more than three key points.
- You should illustrate each point with evidence and examples.

c. **Summary/ending** – *'Tell them what you've told them.'*

- End with a strong summary of the purpose and the key points.

- The last two sentences are what people will remember – make sure they're worthy.
- The ending should also be attention grabbing but not so much that it brings up new questions.
- End with a 'call to action' where possible - something that you want the audience to think or do as a result of your presentation.
- Don't finish with a question or an apology – it would indicate a loss of control.

5. **Create a Script**

   It's important to have a script to start off with so that you're clear about what you want to say. Once you're comfortable with it and have practised reading it out loud, you can then break it down into bullet point reminders that you can use on the day. **DO NOT use a detailed script for the actual presentation.**

How to write a presentation script:

- Say it out loud as you're writing:
  - It forces you to decide on the best order.
  - It enables you to spot where repetition is necessary and where it's harmful.
  - It helps eliminate clichés and jargon.
  - You can check it against your 'statement.'

  - You'll be able to shape the flow and improve the tone.
- Read it for sense.
- Edit for impact.
- **Use humour** where appropriate.

USING HUMOUR

Humour is an excellent way to get your message across and ensure you make an impact – as long as you make an impact for the *right* reasons:

- **Types of humour to avoid**
  - Racism
  - Sexism
  - Cartoons
  - Impersonations
  - Anything that could be deemed as being unprofessional

- **Deliver humour**
  - With precision with confidence
  - With speed
  - With practise

In summary:

- Write out a baseline script using your structure.

- Edit the text.
- Open with an attention grabber.
- Close with a call to action (where possible) or something memorable.
- **Everything must relate back to your statement**, if it doesn't, ditch it or put it in a handout.

6. Develop visual aids

Using visual aids can be tricky. When I refer to visual aids, I mean the presentation software you use as well as props. Nowadays, people are tired of seeing Microsoft PowerPoint presentations especially when they have a poor design or contain too much information.

If you want to use presentation software, a fantastic alternative to PowerPoint or Apple's Keynote (which is available for free, albeit with limited functionality), is Prezi. I now use nothing else for training and presentation purposes, as I find that as it's more engaging that PowerPoint. Audiences tend to pay more attention to Prezi because it's, providing you with the ability to present information in a relatively new and different format, which can be more engaging for the audience.

VISUAL AIDS

When creating visual aids such as presentations in Prezi or PowerPoint, you should bear the following points in mind:

- Only use them to *support* what you're saying.
- They should be a secondary focus; they shouldn't contain the whole presentation or your entire script.
- Use them sparingly – for maximum impact have minimum slides.
- Use them to express, explain or describe.
- They should reinforce the main messages.
- Keep slides simple, bright and leave plenty of white space.
- Pictures and graphics always beat text, especially for the 'visual' audience members.
- Avoid too much animation as its distracting.
- Keep text size and font consistent on each slide (attention to detail is critical).
- Avoid graphs/tables containing too much information.
- Prepare a backup document (just in case there's a problem with the IT).

USING PROPS

- Use 'props' e.g. videos, sound bites, product examples, music, etc. where appropriate to support your presentation. Such accessories are perfect for getting your message across to visual and kinesthetic audience members (I discuss different communications styles later in this chapter).

- Keep props out of sight until they're needed as they can distract the audience. If you leave them in view throughout your presentation, the audience will be distracted, wondering what they're for rather than listening to you.
- Remove props once you've finished with them to lessen the distraction.

N.B. YOU DON'T HAVE TO USE POWERPOINT, KEYNOTE OR PREZI! We are so used to using presentation software that it may not occur to you that you don't have to. If you're confident enough, you can simply talk or use a flip chart. If you decide to do this, my only concern would be how you come across to your 'visual' audience members who respond to visual styles of communication.

7. **Prepare your notes**

When it comes to making notes, there are some 'do's' and 'don'ts':

- **Don't use a detailed script** - If you try to use a detailed script, it's likely that you'll lose your place and become flustered. Using the script you've already prepared, note the key points down on small cards. Make sure you number the cards and find some way of attaching them together in sequence. That way, if you drop them (which I've seen a particularly nervous presenter do), you won't lose your place.

- **Don't use shorthand** – When you're under pressure, it's likely that you won't be able to remember the meaning of something that you've written in shorthand.

- **Type or write your notes in a large font** – Also use adequate spacing between each line, this will make notes easier to read under pressure. Some people like to transfer their presentation notes to an iPad/tablet; be careful if you do that, as you can easily lose your place or swipe to the wrong page. Also, ensure that your tablet is fully charged.

- **Your notes should only be there as a prompt** - When I'm training or giving a presentation, I rarely use notes. I know what I want to say and use the key points on the screen as my prompts to remind me of the order rather than what I should be saying.

- **Don't put all your content on slides and read it out** – If you do this, your presentation will not flow, and the audience will try to read your slides rather than listening to what you're saying.

PRESENTING WITH IMPACT

1. **Practise**
    - **Practise your presentation as many times as possible** both for real and through clear visualisation.
    - Check content and timings.
    - Check that visual aids and props are working.
2. **Control your breathing**
    - Learn to breathe deeply and in a controlled manner - Use the breathing exercise from the next chapter
    - Controlling your breathing helps control nerves and makes it easier for others to understand you
3. **Be aware of your mannerisms**
    - We communicate nerves through our mannerisms
    - Identify what gives your nerves away
    - If you know that you use fillers repeatedly such as *"erm" "like"* or *"you know"* etc., practise taking a breath rather than saying the word. If you actively change those unwanted words for something else or take a breath instead, with consistent practise, you'll eradicate them from your

vocabulary altogether.

- TOP TIP An excellent way to notice unhelpful mannerisms is to video yourself giving your presentation. If you notice something you don't like, make a conscious effort to change it and practise the new way as many times as possible.

4. **Develop a positive attitude**
   - Be aware of your negative 'internal talk.'
   - Negative self-talk can stop you giving a high performance. Remember, *'Thoughts Become Things'* and *'we get what we think about'*. Therefore, think about your presentation only in positive terms.

5. **Visualise**

   'The mind can't tell the difference between something that's vividly imagined and something that's real.'

   - Practise visualising the whole presentation going perfectly. Create a video in your mind, see what you'd see, hear what you'd hear and feel what you'd feel in as much detail as possible. Make it big, bright and noisy and run that video as many times as you possibly can before the big day, as well as just before you present, if possible.
   - Practise is THE biggest best way to halt nerves. Whether

you practise it for real or just in your mind, it has the same effect on your nervous system.

- Use fear as a cattle prod for preparation

6. **Use positive body language to establish rapport:**

- Smile.
- Stand straight.
- Maintain eye contact by scanning the audience, looking the audience in the eye as you do.
- Use positive facial expressions.
- Be open and assertive. Keep your palms on view and use open hand gestures. Hiding your palms, tells others (subconsciously) that you have something to hide.
- Be aware of habits/mannerisms.
- Don't pace; it's distracting.
- Don't stare at one person; you'll make them feel uncomfortable.
- Don't look over people's heads; it freaks audiences out when presenters do that. It makes them wonder what you're looking at towards the back of the room.

7. **Control your voice:**

- **Project your voice without shouting** – You should practise this at home if you're not used to it.
- **Speak slowly** – We tend to speak more quickly when we're nervous. Make a conscious effort to slow down your speech.

- **Vary tone, volume, and speed** – Try to inject as much life into your voice as possible keeping delegates thoroughly engaged.
- **Pronounce words distinctly** – Don't mumble, you want people to hear and understand what you're saying.
- **Use pauses** – Often pausing in the right place can be quite dramatic. Pause where you want the audience to think about what you've just stated.

Other top tips:

1. **Let the room settle down** – Wait for the audience to settle before you start, ensuring that you have everyone's attention.

2. **Practise saying your first line** – Your first line sets the tone for the rest of the presentation. Practise cutting out the fillers e.g. *"OK," "so," "right"*.

3. **Be receptive and observe your audience's body language** – I am acutely aware of my audience at all times, and if I feel that they may be drifting (I can tell that by watching their body language, facial expressions and where they rest their eyes), I'll do something unexpected. For example, I'll get them to stand up, or I'll vary the tone of my voice or ask an unexpected question. All these techniques draw the audience's attention back to what I'm saying as it interrupts their current thinking pattern.

4. **Nail your ending** - Your ending is critical; it's what the audience will go away remembering the most. Therefore, make sure that you end on a high rather than letting your presentation fizzle out.

5. **Practise makes perfect** – I can't emphasise this enough. Good quality practise will make a massive difference to your performance on the day.

DEALING WITH QUESTIONS

Questions are an inevitable part of presentations and something many of my clients fear the most. Here are my guidelines for successfully managing this section of your presentation:

- If you have limited time (most interview presentations are time sensitive) tell the audience before you start, that you'll be taking questions at the end. If you do get asked a question when you're mid flow, don't stop to answer it, say, *"I'll answer that at the end if that's OK?"*

- If you get asked a question that you don't know the answer to, don't panic. Say that you'll look into it and provide answers after the presentation. I usually say something like, *"Oh good question. Leave it with me, and I'll get back to you before the end of the day."* Most people will be happy with that.

- If your presentation isn't subject to strict timings, ask if the audience has any questions *before* you give your summary/ending. That way, if you get asked a tricky question, you aren't going to end on a potential negative.

HOW TO ANSWER QUESTIONS

If you use the following guidelines, you will be in control the Q&A rather than letting it control you:

- Always pause before you reply to give yourself some breathing space. This can help stop you from saying the wrong thing.
- Never patronise e.g. *"I'm glad you asked that..."*
- If you don't know the answer, say so.
- If the question isn't relevant or is only applicable to that person, don't be afraid to interrupt and tell them that you'll be happy to answer their question after the presentation.
- If you're unsure what someone means, ask them for clarification.
- Keep answers brief.
- ***Never get defensive***. If you get asked a question and become defensive, it can harm the audience's perception of you. If you feel yourself getting defensive, take a deep breath before answering and consciously *choose* how you reply.

- Beware of getting into too much dialogue and spending too much time answering one question. Take it offline if possible, I usually say something like, *"Do you mind if we pick this up afterwards?"*
- Use the three 'Ss' – **SAY IT. SUPPORT IT. SHUT IT!**

Prepare by writing down all the potential questions you could be asked and how you would answer them. Here are some examples of what you could ask yourself:

- What is the most embarrassing/challenging/appalling question I could be asked?
- What would I ask if I were deeply cynical?
- What would I ask if someone else giving the same presentation?
- What question could expose my greatest weakness?
- What questions would I love the audience to ask?

DESIGNING & DELIVERING PRESENTATIONS

- **Practise, Practise, Practise!** The more you practise, the better you'll become. Public speaking is a set of skills that can be learnt.

- Have no more than three key points in a ten-minute presentation – no more than five key points if you have longer
- *"Tell them what you're going to tell them, tell them and then tell them what you've told them."*
- Use small prompt cards NOT a detailed script – remember to number the cards and fix them together so that if you drop them, you can easily find your place.
- If you use presentation software e.g. Prezi/PowerPoint/ Keynote, have plenty of 'white space' on the screen and make sure you test that everything is working properly.
- Prepare for any possible questions.
- Use positive, open body language.
- Stay on time – practise will help you with that. When I have to stick to time, I take my watch off and put it somewhere so that it can be seen easily without drawing attention to the fact that I'm looking at it.
- Have a glass of water on hand – we often get dry mouth when we're nervous.
- Remember that you know your content; your audience doesn't. Therefore, if you make a mistake, don't admit it, move on – it's unlikely that the audience will notice unless you tell them!

- Video yourself giving your presentation that way you'll be able to see what works and what doesn't. You'll also notice if you have any unhelpful mannerisms which you need to address.
- Visualise your perfect outcome. By frequently imagining a positive outcome, you'll adequately prepare yourself for the real thing.

CHAPTER 7 – INTERVIEW SKILLS

"If you never try, you'll never know."

ON THE DAY

There are some very basic 'dos' and 'don'ts' regarding how to conduct yourself before, during and after an interview. You may think that some of the items I've listed here are a bit basic; however, they are all common mistakes that are regularly made by candidates:

1. **Dress to impress** – How you present yourself is incredibly important when it comes to interviews. Your overall appearance speaks volumes about you, how conscientious and how professional you are. It gives the interviewer a good indication of your personal standards, which you're likely to apply to everything you do.

HOW TO DRESS - MEN

- ALWAYS wear a suit with a shirt and a tie. No matter what role you're applying for whether it is office based or not. If you don't have one, buy one, it's probably one of the best investments you could make. If you spend £100 on a suit, and you land a job that pays you £1000s then that £100 was a great investment.
- The suit should be a dark colour, and the shirt/tie should match but shouldn't be too bright.
- Make sure your clothes are pressed, with no visible creases (that includes the back of your shirt in case you need to take your jacket off!).
- Don't wear cartoon ties or socks – socks should be dark and matching.
- Your shoes should be dark and polished – heels shouldn't be 'down-trodden'.
- Keep jewellery to a minimum (remove any earrings and piercings) and keep tattoos covered, especially if the role is office based.
- Make sure your hair is clean and neat and that you've recently shaved (if you don't have a beard).
- Keep aftershave light – you don't want to overpower the interviewer.
- Your nails should be short, neat and clean.

HOW TO DRESS - LADIES

- You should also wear a suit. Although there has been a distinct decline in women wearing suits over recent years, I think it's still important to wear one at interview. It doesn't matter if it's a skirt, dress or trouser suit as long as it's smart and in darker colours – no bright/pastel colours.
- If you really don't want to wear a suit, you must NOT wear knitwear - knitwear is not smart enough for an interview. Wear a tailored dress or trousers/skirt and a stylish shirt or blouse.
- Ensure your clothes are clean and well pressed. Un-ironed clothes are not acceptable and will make you look sloppy and unprofessional.
- Wear light makeup, (even if you don't usually wear it); just using mascara and lip gloss will make you look more polished. On the other hand, don't overdo it; leave the heavy makeup, false lashes, and bright lipstick for the weekend, as it is a big turn-off for many employers.
- Make sure your nails are neat and tidy, you don't have to have a manicure, but it's great if you do. No chipped polish please and keep nail art to a minimum; you want the interviewers to be focused on you, not on your nails.

- Less is more when it comes to jewellery – no big hoop earrings and statement necklaces. If you wear a long necklace, make sure that you don't fidget with it during the interview as that can be distracting.
- Make sure that your hair is styled and looks neat and well groomed. An 'evening up-do' isn't appropriate for an interview.
- Wear heels if possible even if they are just small ones, and again they should be dark in colour and well polished. **No sandals allowed, not even in summer**. You should wear full shoes or boots only (boots should only be worn in winter). Make sure the heels are not worn down.
- Your perfume shouldn't be overpowering. There's nothing worse for an interviewer than having to sit in a room with someone wearing strong perfume. Not only is it uncomfortable for the recruiter, but it's unpleasant for following candidates to have to smell someone else's lingering scent.
- Keep tattoos covered, especially if the role is office based and remove any obvious piercings (stud earrings are fine).

If you're meeting with a recruitment consultant, you don't necessarily have to wear a full suit (and tie), but as I've mentioned previously, you should NEVER wear jeans. You must always look professional, and I would recommend you still wear a suit.

2. **Arrive ON TIME**

- You should NEVER be late for an interview. If you can't be on time, it says that you're not reliable and that your timekeeping isn't good.
- If you are late, don't make up a false excuse as it's likely that the interviewer will check your story.
- If there is an unavoidable holdup, inform the recruiter as soon as possible. The sooner you tell them, the better it will be for you.
- Do a trial run of getting to the venue and if possible, make sure you do it at the same time and day as your interview. I had one client who ignored this advice and did his trial run into Manchester City Centre on a Sunday afternoon - his interview was 9.00 am on Monday morning. He turned up over an hour late because he hadn't taken rush hour into consideration when planning his journey.
- Always aim to arrive at least 15 minutes early. If you give yourself a bit of extra time, you won't feel rushed or panicked, and you'll have a chance to calm down, collect

your thoughts, take some deep breaths and do your visualisation exercises before your interview starts.

3. **Be nice to the receptionist (and everyone else you meet!)** – If I'm interviewing, I will *always* ask the receptionist how the candidate interacted with them. The way candidates treat the receptionist or the person sent to greet them is a good indicator of their personality and values.

   I'll always remember a director I was managing a recruitment programme with, coming into a pre-interview meeting outraged. Someone had cut him up in the car park, taken a space he was patiently waiting for, and when he challenged him, he was greeted with a tirade of verbal abuse and unacceptable gesturing. It took quite a while and a strong cup of coffee to calm him down. When the candidate walked in the room, can you guess who it was? Not surprisingly, he didn't get the job.

4. **Turn off your mobile phone** - Turn it off as soon as you arrive at the building, this is such simple advice, yet so important, and something many candidates forget to do. Not only is it unprofessional, but it could put you off track if your phone rings when you're in mid flow. It's also very annoying for the interviewer. If you do forget and it does

ring, DO NOT ANSWER IT! Apologise to the interviewer and turn it off immediately.

The same advice is applicable if you're meeting a recruitment consultant. TURN YOUR PHONE OFF. Don't leave it on the table and check it during the meeting if you see a message come through! You'd be surprised how many people do that according to recruitment consultant colleagues - it's unprofessional and rude.)

5. **Be positive – If the interviewer asks you how you are, or** how your journey was, don't complain. Simply say something like, *"Great thanks."* One recruiter was recently telling me that when she asked that question, a candidate replied, *"Well I'm a bit tired and stressed, to be honest."* No recruiter wants to hear that. Be upbeat and positive, even if you aren't feeling it.

6. **Smile, eye contact, strong *dry* handshake** – Nobody likes someone who can't look them in the eye; it's creepy. Even though you may be nervous, it's important to smile and make good eye contact with everyone in the room. Also, use a good strong, dry handshake. Many women (and some men) don't know how to shake hands properly and have developed a light, limp handshake. Non-verbally that says that you are unsure about yourself and your abilities. Many people consider that a limp or light, awkward handshake

indicates a lack of strength of character, therefore, if you know that you don't have a strong handshake, or you feel uncomfortable shaking hands, practise it.

On the reverse, no-one wants to have their hand crushed. It is particularly off-putting when a man squeezes a woman's hand too tight; leaving her hand in pain where her rings have marked her fingers (I'm speaking from experience here!).

7. **In the interview**:

- **Wait to be asked to sit down** - It's polite to wait to be invited.
- **Sit still and comfortably and use positive body language** (see the next section for more on body language) - Sit back in your chair as soon as you sit down, if you 'perch' on the end, there's nowhere for you to go and you'll end up feeling uncomfortable.
- **Don't chew gum** – Seems obvious, but you'd be surprised how many people do it. It's nasty, and it's unprofessional and very off-putting for a recruiter. I remember a client who was perfect for a role; however, the recruiter rejected him because he chewed gum throughout the interview. The interviewer was horrified when he was relaying this to me. When I asked my

client what possessed him to chew gum, he said that when he gets nervous, his mouth can dry up, and he thought chewing gum would alleviate the problem

- **If you're offered a drink, always take it** – If asked whether you would like tea, coffee or water, I suggest accepting water. When we feel under pressure, often our mouths can dry up and, therefore, having water on hand is helpful. If you know you suffer from dry mouth, take a bottle of water in with you. However, don't draw the water through the bottle top as it makes an awful noise. Remove the lid or ask the interviewer for a glass

- **Don't take copious notes** – Its okay to write the odd thing, however, you can't concentrate on what the interviewer is asking while you're busy writing. I find it very distracting if a candidate makes lots of notes in an interview, it's not necessary and contrary to popular belief, it doesn't make you look more professional.

- **Don't apologise for being nervous** – It sets the wrong tone for the interview. Make sure that you do your preparation, breathing exercises and Superman stance (explained later in this chapter) before the interview to control any nerves.

- **Don't fidget** - If you're aware that you fidget either with your hair/pen/necklace etc., remove temptation. It can be very distracting for a recruiter if someone's continually clicking a pen or fiddling with a necklace or security pass.

- **Don't flirt or curse** - I still find it amazing that I have to include this. However, it's happened to me a few times over the years. Men have attempted to flirt with me or have used inappropriate language during an interview. Both are unacceptable and are likely to result in your rejection, no matter how good the rest of your performance is.

- **Make eye contact with EVERYONE in the room** – Don't just address your answers to the person who asked you the question, share your gaze between everyone. If you stare at one person for too long, it can make them feel uncomfortable. If there's a note-taker, look at them too. Just because they have their head down doesn't mean that they can't feel you looking at them.

- **Never underestimate the note-taker** – I was once interviewing with two directors to fill a board director vacancy. I was taking the interview notes for no other reason than the fact that I'm good at it. During the interview, I asked a few questions, and the interviewee (a man) proceeded to direct his answers to the other two (male) directors and completely ignored me. All I can assume is that he thought that because I was a woman, I was only there in a note-taking capacity (despite the fact he had been told my role at the beginning of the interview). Do you think he got the job? Absolutely not! We took his behaviour to indicate that he was both sexist and overly status-conscious; neither of which were acceptable traits within our organisation.

- **Don't be overly confident (arrogant)** - Nobody likes arrogance, and there's a fine line between confidence and arrogance.

- **Don't get too personal or familiar** – This can be a problem when you know one of the interviewers; it can become uncomfortable for them if you are too personal. It's also crucial to still give full answers using the STAR format, especially in a competency based interview. I've know candidates fail because they assumed that the interviewer knew what they'd done, and mistakenly thought that they didn't need to explain themselves. In a competency based interview, if you don't say it, they can't mark it. Whether you know the interviewer or not, is irrelevant.

- Alternatively, if you're the type of person who builds rapport quickly, and you find yourself in synergy with one/all of your interviewers, don't get lulled into a false sense of security and let your guard down. Remain professional at all times.

- **Tell the truth; lies will be found out** – Luckily it's only happened to me once, but I interviewed a candidate who unbeknown to me, had lied on his CV and continued to lie about his skills and achievements during the interview. I offered him the job because I had no reason to believe that what he wasn't truthful. Not long after he started, it became apparent that he didn't have the skills or the experience necessary for the role and subsequently he was dismissed.

- I've witnessed an unusual phenomenon when it comes to interviews; people will say absolutely anything to get a role ... even if they don't want it, or they don't have the skills to be able to do it! Please don't do this as you will only harm yourself and your credibility in the long run.

- **Speak in only positive terms about your current role and employer** – Do not be disrespectful or complain about your current employer, no matter how disgruntled you are or how badly you think you've been treated. No company will employ you if you do. It's unprofessional, and it will make you look like a complainer/troublemaker.

- To illustrate this point, during interview preparation with a client, I explained to her the importance only saying constructive things about her previous employer. I was concerned about how she may come across as she had been made redundant and was feeling disgruntled about her perceived mistreatment by the company.

- She called me after an interview and said, *"I think I've blown it. I launched into how horrible the redundancy process was and what I really thought about the company and how they treated me."* She was right; she had blown it. She didn't get the job even though she thought she'd done well with everything else. When she called the company for feedback (something I urge all my clients to do), they confirmed that she failed because of her attitude.

- **Don't 'blag' or bluff your way through** – Interviewers are rarely looking for the finished article. If you don't know how to do something, tell the truth but explain how you would go about addressing the development area or finding out the information.

- **Avoid using 'we'** – Overusing the word 'we' e.g. *"we arranged", "we provided," "we delivered"* can make an interviewer think that you can only achieve as part of a team or worse, that you were lying about your achievements on your CV.

- **Remember to BREATHE and be POSITIVE**! I'd also add that you should be enthusiastic as it's easy to interpret a lack of passion for a lack of interest.

- **Remember to SMILE**! When we smile, it not only helps us feel better but produces an automatic smile response in others, making them feel better too.

- **The interview isn't over until you've left the premises** – Wait to make any phone calls until you're out of earshot, you never know who's listening/watching. Wait until you're in your car or well away from the building.

COMMUNICATION SKILLS & RAPPORT BUILDING

Your overall communication skills are critical throughout the assessment process; however, I want first to concentrate on your physiology. Physiology encompasses your body language, facial expressions and paralinguistics i.e. *how* we say things (our pitch/tone, etc.).

The largest part of how we communicate is not through the words we use, but through our physiology and paralinguistics which are mainly driven by our subconscious. Figure 4 shows the percentage difference between how the words we use, our body language and paralinguistics contribute towards our overall communication.

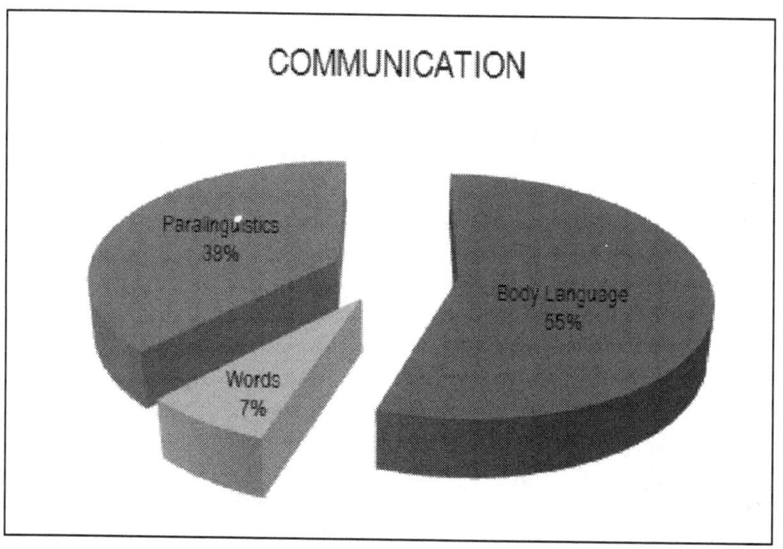

FIGURE 4

As you can see, words are only 7% of what we 'say.' Therefore, it's important that what we communicate through our body language, facial expressions, tone, speed and pitch of our voices is consistent with our words; they must be congruent.

To do this, you need to use positive physiology:

1. Don't cross your arms, even if you're cold, as it indicates that you are closed, uncomfortable, and an interviewer could perceive it as you being hostile.

2. Don't put your hands behind your head. That suggests arrogance.

3. Crossed legs are fine; however, your feet should be pointing towards the interviewer(s). Whether you're sitting or standing, where you position your feet is a good indicator of where you subconsciously want to go; if they are pointing towards the door, then that's a giveaway as to where you'd rather be i.e. out of the door!

4. Keep your hands on your lap and use open-palmed gestures. Open palms signify that you have nothing to hide and is where the term, 'showing your hand' originates. If you hide your palms/hands, the other person will subconsciously think that you have something to hide.

5. Sit up straight in your chair and lean slightly forward, which signifies that you're interested and attentive. Leaning backwards, subconsciously communicates that you don't want to be there, and you're uncomfortable or possibly arrogant.

I once interviewed a candidate who was so laid back that he was almost horizontal in his chair. That gave me the impression that he wasn't interested in the job, that he thought himself too good for it and didn't care whether he got it or not.

6. Smile and nod in agreement in the right places so that the interviewer can see that you're fully engaged.

7. Pay attention to the pace/speed and tone of your voice. When we're nervous, we have a tendency to talk more quickly and at a slightly higher pitch (men as well as women). Therefore, consciously slow your speech down – I suggest you try this when you practise your STAR examples or presentation. If in doubt, a top tip is to mimic the tonality and pace of the interviewer. By doing that, you'll also be subconsciously building great rapport with them.

8. Don't talk over the interviewer as it can be irritating. Wait until they've finished speaking before you reply. I know that can be hard to do when you're keen to get your point across and to show that you're in agreement. However, it can be very frustrating for the other person, and if you don't hear the full question or statement, you may say something inappropriate or that's not pertinent.

9. Subtly mirror the body language of the primary interviewer. By doing that, you'll be subconsciously creating excellent rapport.

There's a section in my first book *'Thoughts Become Things'* about how to build rapport using your physiology, which is an essential influencing technique.

ADJUST YOUR COMMUNICATION STYLE

You also need to consider the interviewers' communication styles. People generally interpret the world in one of three ways:

- What they see (visual)
- What they hear (auditory)
- What they feel (kinesthetic).

We all have a combination of all three styles; however, we do tend to have a preference. Therefore, to make yourself understood during an interview, you need to address each of the three different styles. Here's how you might do it according to each style:

1. **Visual** - 'Show' that you've done your preparation by preparing a professional looking folder containing pertinent information. Also, ensure that you're smartly dressed and well groomed. If you're giving a presentation, include pictures and charts and use plenty of white space.

2. **Auditory** - 'Explain' your answers clearly and without waffling. That's where the STAR preparation comes into play. Using the STAR format ensures that your answers are succinct, and your answers don't drift.

3. **Kinesthetic** - Use appropriate physiology (body language, facial expressions, etc.). Make sure your body language is open and that you make good eye contact. Create rapport by nodding and using appropriate facial expressions.

WHAT TO TAKE INTO AN INTERVIEW

You should always take a professional looking folder with you. You can get them quite cheaply from stationers or even the stationery section at your large local supermarket. The faux leather style that is open on three sides is perfect, or if you want to splash out, a genuine leather one, I'd advise the latter for senior management positions. DO NOT use a tatty old looking paper folder or regular notepad with your notes clumsily stuffed inside, that won't impress anyone.

Why should you use a professional looking folder? For the 'visual' interviewer - I'm a visual person, therefore, if someone turns up at an interview without outwardly 'showing' me that they've prepared, I won't be impressed. I'll assume that they haven't done any preparation. Therefore, having something as simple as a folder containing relevant information will take care of that issue for interviewers with a visual preference.

TOP TIP

If you're an auditory (hearing) or kinesthetic (feeling) person, it may never occur to you do to this, but it's important because you don't know which of the three preferences your interviewer(s) will have. It's one of the small things that can make a big difference.

Your folder should contain:

1. **Two copies of your CV** – You *must* take copies of your CV with you especially if you either completed an application form when applied for the role or if you got the interview through a recruitment consultant. If you completed an application form, then it's beneficial to let the recruiter see how good your CV is. If you applied through a recruitment consultant, it's likely that will have re-designed your CV in their standard format which may not do your CV justice. Also, there have been times when I've had interviews, and the interviewer has forgotten to bring a copy of my CV with them. Having your own copies shows that you prepare and anticipate future needs.

2. **Your achievements in the STAR format** – The bulleted examples of your achievements with two on each sheet of A4 or each one separate on individual cards, with the associated competency clearly written at the top of each.

3. **Your typed questions for the interviewer.**

4. **A copy of the company's competencies** (if applicable) – You should include this especially if you're going to an assessment centre. If you're allowed to have it with you, then you should refer to it throughout the day to ensure that you stay on track.

5. **Copies of significant information from the recruiter's website or from your research** – I recently had a meeting with a prospective client (I prepare for such meetings in much the same way as I would for an interview). During my research on their website, I came across an interesting document that I thought may be useful. I printed off a copy and put it in my folder intending to ask them about it if there was time. During the meeting, I was making notes, and the client saw the copy of their document in my folder and was impressed that I'd gone to the trouble of printing it.

6. **Copies of qualifications** – This is essential if you're a school/college/university leaver. They aren't usually

required otherwise, but if they are, you'll be informed before the interview.

7. **Examples of your work** – Again, I'd advise this if you're a school/college/university leaver as you aren't likely to have much relevant experience from which to draw. I'd also suggest this if you're applying for a creative or professional role e.g. architect, marketing executive, designer, etc. It's likely that a prospective employer would want to see copies of your work as part of the interview.

MANAGING NERVES

The overriding reason people give for failing interviews is 'nerves' and it's usually top of the agenda for most delegates who attend our outplacement programmes. In this section, I'll give you some great tools and techniques for managing your nerves. However, you don't want to remove them totally as they serve an important purpose; they help you perform at a higher level. When we are nervous, we produce adrenaline which contributes towards increased performance. The important thing is to manage the nerves so that they don't get out of control, causing and adverse effect.

MANAGING INTERVIEW NERVES

1. **Do your preparation** – One reason for interview nerves is because we feel out of control. Most people are under the misapprehension that they don't know what questions they will be asked, which can lead to experiencing negative emotions. Hopefully, by now, you've realised that it's not true; you *do* know. You will be asked to demonstrate your achievements, skills, and experience, as well as what you know about the company. Therefore, it's incredibly important to prepare adequately by completing the following activities:

   - Write down and practise saying your achievements out loud using the STAR format.
   - Prepare your answers for the top frequently asked questions.
   - Do your research on the company.
   - Know the competencies you will be assessed against (if applicable).
   - Plan your quality questions for the interviewer.
   - Prepare the relevant information to take to the interview with you.
   - Practise visualising everything going well.

   This amount of preparation covers 80-85% of what you'll get asked at an interview. I know it seems like a lot of work, however, *'we get out what we put in.'* I find that clients who follow this advice find that their nerves almost disappear, leaving only a healthy amount.

2. **Breathe deeply** - When we become stressed or anxious, our breathing tends to become shallower. The following is an excellent exercise that you can use to control your breathing, making yourself instantly feel better. It calms and relaxes the body and mind; the good thing about it is that no-one knows you're doing it, and you can do it anywhere:

DEEP BREATHING

1. Take ten deep breaths:
    - In and out counts as one breath
    - Breathe in through the nose/out through the mouth
2. While breathing deeply, think of something you find calming e.g. a beautiful beach, walking in the countryside, etc.
3. Repeat as necessary

Once you reach around six/seven breaths, physiological changes occur in the body: feel good hormones (endorphins) are released that counteract the stress hormone (cortisol) which the body releases when we're feeling stressed.

3. **Visualise the outcome you want** – I've already talked about the importance of visualisation. Don't forget to read the section at the back of this book that gives you more information about how to visualise effectively.

4. **Act like a superhero!** - We've all heard the term *'Fake it 'til you make it'* and there is now evidence that supports that this actually works when we change our physiology. We can trick our brains into producing different emotions by purposefully changing our body language to that of the emotion that we want to experience. Even better than that is the fact that not only can we change our mood, but we can influence hormone release (our biochemistry) by changing our physiology.

   Recent research has confirmed that adopting a 'power stance' (think of a superhero posture, legs spread, hands on hips, elbows bent and chin up) conveys a sense of the individual having power. Furthermore, tests have proven that adopting this stance for two minutes affects our release of the hormones testosterone and cortisol. Why these two hormones?

- ***Testosterone*** - Research on testosterone in relation to power indicates that testosterone levels increase when we anticipate competing (it's the same for men and women), as well as after winning, but testosterone levels drop when we lose. In other words, testosterone goes up with the possibility of, or with actual power and decreases when power, or the opportunity to attain power, is lost.

- ***Cortisol*** - Sometimes referred to as a 'stress hormone' because its levels often rise with stress. People who are powerful or hold powerful positions tend to have lower baseline levels of cortisol and, when stressed, their cortisol levels don't rise as much as in people who are relatively powerless or *perceive* that they are.

INCREASE YOUR POWER

Whenever you want to increase your power e.g. your confidence and self-esteem, etc. you simply need to do this exercise to trick your mind and body into actually experiencing physiological changes which will supercharge your performance:

1. Stand up tall with your feet part.
2. Put your hands on your hips.
3. Tighten your stomach muscles.
4. Put your shoulders back and push your chest out
5. Lift your chin.

6. Take a deep breath and say, *"I'm magnificent!"*
7. If you can, actually walk around making big confident strides (you could even imagine a Superhero cape on your back if you like!).
8. Hold this stance for two minutes and you'll have no option but to feel more powerful as your physiology will automatically change your biochemistry.

I appreciate that you may feel a little silly doing this, but it does work, and all the research is there to back it up, just Google 'Superman Stance.' I teach this to clients who would like to feel more confident in challenging conditions such as interviews, presentations or public speaking. I urge them to go to the washroom (if there isn't anywhere else that they can be alone) and stand in a cubical for two minutes doing the 'Superhero Stance.' OK, it may not be the best venue, but the results will be the same; you'll feel more confident and positive.

Stand like a superhero, feel like a superhero, act like a superhero!

AFTER THE INTERVIEW

Make a note of what went well and what you think could be improved upon. Do it as soon as you can after afterwards so that it's still fresh in your mind. The reason for doing this is so that you can objectively review your development areas and make any necessary adjustments for your next interview.

I know that doing this exercise can be uncomfortable for some, especially if you're particularly self-critical; however, it's important for your future performance. Most good companies will provide feedback although it won't be top of their priority list and therefore, you may need to remind them. If you went for the role through a recruitment consultant, they should be able to give you feedback on behalf of their client.

Remember not to take feedback as a negative; although it may feel like it, it's not personal. Take any learning points and incorporate them into your preparation for your next interview/assessment centre.

CHAPTER 8 – JOB OFFER

"Don't base your decisions on the advice of those who don't have to live with the consequences."

There's nothing like the feeling you get when you finally get offered a job that you really want. However, it's important that the offer fits with (a) what you were expecting (b) what you need.

Most offers are made subject to certain 'conditions'; this is a 'conditional offer'. These conditions almost always include the receipt of acceptable references and can also include a satisfactory medical and receipt of appropriate documentation. For example, eligibility to work in the UK, copy of your UK driving license (if the role involves driving on company business), copies of qualifications, etc. Therefore, don't be surprised if the recruiter tells you that they are making a 'conditional offer.'

There are some key details to think about before you accept; the first thing to look for is whether the contract reflects the discussions you had at interview. Are you happy with the overall package including the pay and benefits? It's not uncommon for an employer to discuss the terms at the interview, only for the formal offer to contain contrary information. Therefore, make sure you check the contract carefully before signing it and only sign when you're completely happy.

NEGOTIATING THE TERMS

Once you've received a formal offer, you're in a strong position to negotiate your terms e.g. salary, benefits, start/end times, working days, etc. This is especially important for senior management and professional/technical roles because the pay structure and needs of the business are likely to be more fluid. At the point of offer, a company will have invested a considerable amount time and money on the recruitment process and therefore, may to be open to some level of negotiation to secure you. If the role is a 'hard to fill' and there isn't a ready pool of candidates to choose from, your bargaining position increases significantly.

However, there is a fine line between asking for what you want and pushing too hard. Pushing too hard and being unreasonable is likely to upset the prospective employer and could ruin the relationship before it's started. I've experienced candidates doing this; it's not professional, and it's not a good way to start. If a candidate has pushed too hard, to the point where I think they're unreasonable, with agreement from the hiring manager, I will withdraw the offer. Therefore, if you decide to negotiate your package aggressively, proceed with caution.

A good example of this was one particular candidate who had gone through a strict selection process for a specialist IT role. He had all the necessary skills and experience and scored the highest during the selection process. When I called to offer him the position, he came back with a long list of demands despite the fact that I had stipulated the details of the package very clearly in the first interview. He knew he was in an excellent position and was determined to make the most of it.

We began negotiating, but he kept changing his demands with each conversation. It became incredibly frustrating for the hiring manager and me – no-one likes to feel that they're being held to ransom. What the candidate didn't know was that the runner-up was only one point behind him (most companies never reject the runners up until an offer has been formally accepted by the preferred candidate, that way, they have a fallback position if they need it). After over a week of negotiations and his ever-changing demands, he still hadn't accepted the offer. I discussed the situation with the hiring manager, and we made the joint decision to withdraw the offer, knowing from experience that if he is hard to work with at the job offer stage, it was a good indicator that he would be intolerable once in the post.

NEGOTIATING YOUR CONTRACT

1. **Be realistic** – I do advise people to try to increase their salary as they move between companies; otherwise, it can be difficult to progress up the ladder (if that's what you want to do). However, I don't recommend that you ask for more than £5,000 on top of what you're currently earning. If you go much higher than that, it's likely that the role will require a greater degree of skill or more experience than you may currently have. The leap from where you are now to where you want to be may be too far. I do know people who've done just that and have struggled in the new role – that's not right for you or your new employer. Go with what makes you feel comfortable.

   N.B. the only ways a new company can find out your current salary are:

   - **By looking at your P45** – A P45 is the document that you receive when your employment ends with your current employer and it shows your earnings to date for that financial year. I've only known one manager check a new employee's P45 against the salary they stated at interview.

     The P45 showed a lower salary than what the

employee had claimed she was earning. The hiring manager confronted her, and she explained that she had a pay rise a couple of months previously, and as it was part way through the year, it wasn't reflected in her P45. That explanation is perfectly reasonable.

People think that if they don't provide their P45, then they will be placed on an emergency tax code (a higher rate of tax), which is true. However, if you complete a P46, you will not pay the higher tax rate and the company won't need your P45.

- **From a previous employer reference** – This is highly unlikely as businesses tend only to give the bare minimum of information on references for fear of litigation.

2. **Don't expect a higher rate for hourly paid jobs** – Non-management, hourly paid roles such as warehouse operatives, telesales, administrators, shop workers, cleaners and many public sector organisations tend to have a set hourly rate or salary. It's worth a try, but it it's unlikely that you'll be able to negotiate a higher rate.

3. **'Trade-off' where necessary** – A company will be more willing to accommodate your requests if there's some give and take. Think about the things that are important to you (revisit the 'Get Clear' list you made earlier – see Chapter 2) and trade off the

less valuable items for the things that are important to you. For example, having your employer pay for private medical insurance for you and your family may be more important than having the latest BMW.

TOP TIP

4. **Don't start with the new company if you aren't happy with the terms** – Most people don't realise that you don't have to sign a contract for it to become binding. Once you start work, it will be deemed that you have accepted the terms and conditions stated in the contract. Therefore, it's advisable to iron out any contractual issues *before* you start as there won't be much impetus for the company to do it afterwards.

Apart from the obvious salary, hours, holidays, etc., you may wish to consider negotiating the following:

1. **Health and personal injury insurance** - Often where the benefit is only available for the employee, it's possible to negotiate cover for the whole family.

2. **Car or car allowance** – If your role entails a significant amount of travelling or if you are entitled to a 'status' car or car allowance, it may be possible to negotiate either more money or a better car. If you know that you do a large

number of personal miles, it may also be worth asking for personal fuel allowance. Check with an accountant or independent financial advisor as to whether fuel allowance for personal use would be beneficial for you (unless you do a lot of private miles, you can end up paying more in tax than the benefit is worth).

3. **Other benefits** – Read your contract carefully and look for areas where you may be able to negotiate up to a better package.

4. **Restrictive covenants** – If you're in a sales/professional/ management/senior management role it's likely that you'll be bound by restrictive covenants. These are designed to stop you from resigning and going straight to a competitor, taking sensitive information with you e.g. clients, intellectual property or even your colleagues. Consider whether the covenants are reasonable, especially the timescales. If they seem unreasonable, consult an employment lawyer as they could potentially hinder future employment prospects.

5. **Probationary periods** – Check to see what the probationary period is in your contract. If you think it's too long, again, you may wish to see if it's possible to negotiate it to a more acceptable level.

6. **Notice periods** – Notice periods is an interesting one. Clients will often complain to me that the notice period in their new contract is too long. They express concern about the length of time they'll have to work if they resign after finding another job. However, I see a long notice period as a benefit, as it gives you more protection if the company wishes to terminate your employment as they will have to pay you for your full notice period (unless you are dismissed for gross misconduct).

If you decide to leave, most notice periods are negotiable anyway. Companies don't tend to want employees in a role for a prolonged period following their resignation unless they are in a critical or hard to replace position. However, even if that's the case, negotiating an early leave date may still be possible.

UTILISING YOUR RECRUITMENT CONSULTANT

When it comes to negotiating your contract, having a good relationship with your recruitment consultant is invaluable. Negotiating is part of their key responsibilities, and therefore, they should have no problem in helping you get the best possible deal. However, as I've already mentioned, don't be too demanding, as you'll not only upset the recruiter but the consultant too. Be clear but realistic about what it is that you want, and they should be willing to negotiate on your behalf. In most cases, it's in their best interest to secure a high salary for you as it will directly affect their commission payment based on the fee for placing you.

TOP TIP

DO NOT STOP YOUR JOB SEARCH UNTIL YOU HAVE RECEIVED, SIGNED AND RETURNED YOUR CONTRACT. Many people stop their job search as soon as they receive a verbal offer (or even worse, when they get the interview) choosing not to apply for further roles or go for other interviews. Calling a halt to your search is a mistake; anything can happen between the verbal offer and receiving/signing the paperwork.

This advice is particularly important if you're out of work. You can't afford to halt your job search activities. If you do, and something goes wrong, you will have wasted valuable time and potentially some great opportunities.

THE PAPERWORK

THE EMPLOYMENT CONTRACT

Employment contracts (sometimes referred to as a 'Contract of Employment' or 'Statement of Terms & Conditions') are legal documents provided to you by your employer, outlining the terms of the employer/employee relationship. Employees are legally entitled to a Written Statement of the principal terms and conditions of employment within two calendar months of starting work, and it should include details of things like pay, holidays and working hours.

TOP TIP **Make sure that you read the contract very carefully *before* you sign as they often contain mistakes.**

Employment law experts usually design template employment contracts, which are drawn up for each new employee by the HR/admin department. The hiring manager will pass the information to HR (or whoever prepares the paperwork) who then populates the relevant template. There's a lot of room for error in this process. Therefore, **you must check that what you were verbally offered and agreed to is reflected in the contract**. If it doesn't match, phone the company immediately and ask them to change it to what was verbally agreed.

TOP TIP **DO NOT RESIGN FROM YOUR CURRENT EMPLOYER UNTIL YOU'VE RECEIVED, ARE HAPPY WITH, HAVE SIGNED AND RETURNED YOUR CONTRACT.**

I can't emphasise this enough. I've heard so many horror stories of people resigning from their current employer only for the new job to fall through, and a contract never materialise. They've then gone back to the current employer and tried to withdraw their resignation, however, the company has declined, leaving them without a job. Protect yourself; don't let that happen to you, even if the new business promises you that it's 'in the post.' Wait until you have it in your hands, and you're happy with it before you resign, no matter how frustrating it may be.

MEDICAL & OCCUPATIONAL HEALTH

Some companies will want you to attend a medical which is general practice in larger organisations. Medicals protect the company and are often required by insurers, especially for senior management/ board director positions.

Even if you aren't asked to attend a medical, it's likely that you will be required to complete an 'occupational health questionnaire,' declaring any underlying medical reasons why you may not be able to fulfill your duties. They will also want to know if you have a registered disability. N.B. It's unlawful for a company not to employ you on these grounds, without good reason. They have a legal obligation to make 'reasonable adjustments' to the workplace and your work if that's the case. However, there may be genuine reasons not to employ you e.g. if the role involves lots of heavy lifting and you have a diagnosed degenerative back problem which could be exacerbated as a result of carrying your daily duties.

After seeking medical advice, they may be within their rights to retract their offer.

Be honest about any illnesses or disabilities either during a medical, on any paperwork or when asked. A company may not be able to discriminate against you during the selection process, however, if you have a disability/illness, and you don't declare it when asked, they can dismiss you for 'falsification of company documents' if it later comes to light.

RIGHT TO WORK

It's a legal requirement for employers to check an applicant's employment status prior to starting work. The company must ensure that their employees have the right documentation to be able to work in the UK. They could face a civil penalty if they employ an illegal worker and haven't carried out the correct right to work checks.

When you present your documents, a company will check:

1. The documents you provide are genuine, original and unchanged and belong to you.
2. The dates for your right to work in the UK haven't expired.
3. Photographs are the same across all documents and look like you.

4. Dates of birth are the same across all documents.

5. You have permission to do the type of work the company is offering (including any limit on the number of hours you can work).

6. For students, they need to see evidence of your study and holiday times.

7. If you provide two documents which give different names, that you have evidence showing why they're different, e.g. a marriage certificate or divorce decree.

If you are unable to supply these documents, the employer may ask the Home Office to check your immigration employment status if one of the following applies:

- They're reasonably satisfied that you can't show your documents because of an outstanding appeal, administrative review or application with the Home Office.
- You have an Application Registration Card.
- You have a Certificate of Application that is less than six months old.

The Home Office will send the employer a 'Positive Verification Notice' to confirm that you have the right to work.

The employer must:

- See the original documents.
- Check that the papers are valid with the applicant present.
- Make and keep copies of the documents and a record of the date that they were checked.

ACCEPTABLE DOCUMENTS FOR RIGHT TO WORK CHECKS

A full list of accepted documents is available from the Home Office website at www.gov.uk/. The most commonly accepted include:

- Full UK Birth and Adoption Certificates.
- UK passport.
- EU passport or national identity card.
- A Registration Certificate or Document Certifying Permanent Residence.
- A Permanent Residence Card.
- A current Biometric Immigration Document.

If you can't provide this information, an employer has the right to withdraw their offer of employment. A job offer will always be conditional on you being able to prove your eligibility to work in the UK.

QUALIFICATIONS

Some companies may ask to see copies of your qualifications or may wish to check your professional status i.e. your membership with professional bodies such as the CIPD, ACCA, BPS, CIB, CIMA, etc.

DRIVING LICENSE

A company will want to see your original driving license (not a copy) if you will be driving as part of your role and they are providing you either permanently or temporarily with a company car or car allowance.

REFERENCES

Most companies will ask for a minimum of two references; both should be from your current and previous employers. However, it may not always be possible to provide two work references:

1. **If you've only worked at one company** – In that case, give the reference details for that company plus a personal referee. That should be someone who holds a professional role, is a manager, business owner or someone of standing in the community (e.g. priest/doctor) and who has known you for some years.

2. **If this is your first job** – Your school, college or university should be able to provide you with a reference. You may also be asked to supply a personal reference too.

I must be honest here; many references aren't worth the paper that they're written on. Most companies will only provide the barest minimum of information which must be factual and be able to be evidenced. That's because if a company provides information that adversely affects an employee's/ex-employee's future employment, they could be open to litigation.

With this in mind, most companies will only provide references containing the following information:

- The dates you worked for the organisation
- The job title you had upon leaving
- Your reason for leaving

When I managed HR functions, I wouldn't allow any other information to be included in references, nor would I let anyone else other than HR to supply them on company headed paper. All references had to come from HR, to safeguard the business and minimise potential legal claims.

You can, however, ask a manager to provide you with a personal reference, but it's likely that they will be reluctant to comment on your work or mention the company name directly, preferring to comment on your personal qualities.

Choose your referees carefully. There's nothing to stop a prospective employer from calling your referees directly and asking them for a verbal reference. Referees will usually be much more candid in a conversation and could tell the caller things about you that they would never put in writing.

TOP TIP

Provide reference information promptly. The longer you leave it, the more suspicious the company will become. Remember that most job offers are conditional on receiving two satisfactory references; therefore, if the company doesn't receive them promptly, without good reason, they may consider terminating your employment, even if you've already started working for them.

MAKING THE RIGHT CHOICE

Using your gut feeling or intuition is, without a doubt, the best indicator of whether you're making the right decision or not. If you are offered a job that on paper it looks fantastic, but your gut feeling is telling you that it's wrong, then it probably is. Your gut feeling is there for a reason; it's an inbuilt protection tool designed to keep you safe.

It may be that you just need some more information or to visit the company again to feel more comfortable before you make a decision. If that's the case, contact the recruiter and ask to meet the team with whom you would be working; that way, you will get a feel for what it's like to work there. If the company has nothing to hide and they want you for the job, they shouldn't have a problem with it, so don't be afraid to ask. The job and company have to be right for you, every bit as much you have to be right for them.

TOP TIP Don't take the first thing that comes along if it doesn't feel right. If you can afford to wait a little longer, then you should. The elation of finding a job and being able to pay the mortgage and bills etc. only lasts for a maximum of three months, after that, the reality of having to do that job day in day out sets in.

TOP TIP **It has to be your decision**. It's fine to get advice and guidance from others (friends, colleagues, family members, etc.). However, you must remember that they will have their own agenda and will be processing *your* information through *their* filters. They aren't you; they don't have your skills, your experience, your knowledge, your courage, your drive and therefore, aren't ideally placed to tell you what to do, no matter how well they think they know you. By all means listen to what they have to say, but make your own decision. Don't live your life for someone else; it's you that will have live with the consequences.

RESIGNING FROM YOUR CURRENT EMPLOYER

When you resign from your current employer, be as professional as possible. The last thing you want to do is burn any bridges and leave on a bad note. Employees move from company to company all the time, especially within the same industry or profession, so there's a good chance that you could end up working with the same people again in the future. Unfortunately, there's also the slim chance that something could go wrong, and you may need to ask for your current job back.

As we've discussed, offers are usually conditional upon medicals and references, etc. also company circumstances can change resulting in the company retracting their offer. So you can't afford to upset your current employer in case you need to stay. Make sure that you put your resignation, politely, in writing. An example of a resignation letter is available at the back of the book under 'Additional Resources'.

WHAT TO DO IF YOU GET A COUNTER OFFER

If you are in a critical role or are well liked by your current company, it's common for them to make a counter offer; usually tempting you more money, increased benefits, promotion or the promise of a better work/life balance if you stay. This is sometimes referred to as 'buy back'. It's often in the company's best interests to try and keep you for the following reasons:

- The high recruitment costs associated with replacing you.
- The loss of continuity and history.
- The potential loss of revenue during the recruitment process and the new hire's probationary period.

If you receive a counter offer, here's a startling statistic that may make you think twice about accepting:

After accepting a counter offer, nine out of ten employees leave their current employer within six months.

Be clear about the reasons why you decided to look elsewhere in the first place. People rarely leave their current job just because of pay. It's likely that the problems that prompted you to move in the first place will still be there no matter what they offer you to stay.

WHAT TO DO IF A JOB OFFER GETS RETRACTED

There are three main reasons why companies withdraw offers:

1. Change in business priorities. Unfortunately, the business world is still very volatile, and it doesn't look like it's settling down anytime soon. Despite the fact that we are obviously no longer in the depths of a recession, there are still plenty of companies downsizing or restructuring due to changes in business priorities, decreasing turnover/sales, removal of

government funding, etc. and which can often result in recruitment freezes.

2. The company unexpectedly receives/finds out information about the new hire which casts doubt on their employability e.g. undesirable information on social media. If this happens to you, the company has to be able to prove it; otherwise, you could claim that their reason was unlawful. Contact ACAS (The Advisory, Conciliation and Arbitration Service, a free service that is available to both employers and employees - their details can are in the 'References' section of this book) or an employment lawyer to check the legalities of your individual situation.

3. There are elements of the 'conditional offer' are unfulfilled, e.g. the company receives an unsatisfactory reference or medical report. If this is the case, you have little recourse the contract clearly stated that the offer was conditional.

KNOW YOUR RIGHTS

DISCRIMINATION

In the UK, it's unlawful for a company to withdraw an offer which could be classed as discriminatory if you have a 'protected characteristic', for example:

- Your age

- Being or becoming a transsexual person
- Being married or in a civil partnership
- Being pregnant or having a child
- If you have a registered disability
- Your race including colour, nationality, ethnic or national origin
- Your religion, belief or lack of religion/belief
- Your sex
- Your sexual orientation

If your offer is retracted and you believe the basis for the decision was a protected characteristic (ideally you'll have evidence), then you could consider taking legal action.

IF YOU MEET ALL THE CONTRACTUAL CONDITIONS...

To be told that your new job is no longer available can be devastating, especially if you've already resigned from your current role. If you have signed and returned your contract of employment, the new employer has to formally terminate the contract. If they don't, it will be a breach of contract, and you could consider taking legal action.

Your loss in respect of such a breach will usually only begin to accrue after the date on which your employment was due to start. For example, if you had a four week notice period, but the employer wrongfully terminated your contract one week before you were due to start work, there would normally be a limit on damages of three weeks' earnings.

IF YOU DIDN'T MEET THE CONTRACTUAL CONDITIONS...

If you didn't meet the conditions or the company found something out about you that was undesirable, then, unfortunately, there's nothing that you can do about it. If you had a contract, it's likely that it will have clearly stated that the offer was conditional, and therefore, there's nothing you can do unless you have evidence that the retraction was because of something covered by a protected characteristic. If the company withdraws the offer because of something on your social media, make sure that you remedy it immediately.

IF YOU'VE ALREADY RESIGNED

If you've already resigned, and the offer gets retracted, arrange a meeting with your line manager as soon as possible and explain the situation. If you have a good relationship with your employer, and you've been professional during your resignation/notice period and if they haven't already replaced you, they may allow you to stay. However, the company has no legal obligation to keep you once they've accepted your resignation. They may consider that the 'psychological contract' has been broken, and, as a result, are happy to let you go. If you aren't able to stay with your current employer, then you need to start the job hunt process again, immediately.

WHAT TO DO IF YOU CHANGE YOUR MIND

Once you start your job hunting in earnest, it's possible that you could receive two or more job offers at the same time. If you've already formally accepted one, and get offered something more suitable, don't be afraid withdraw from the original. Make sure you do it in a professional manner by telephoning and following up your decision in writing. It's annoying and discourteous when a candidate withdraws by sending an email or a text.

It's far better to turn a company down than end up in the wrong job and thinking *"What if?"* for the rest of your life. Although I do appreciate that this can feel unprofessional. Try not to base your choice solely on money; you should consider where you'll be happiest and can make the most difference doing something you enjoy. If you do withdraw your acceptance, don't be surprised if they come back with a counter offer. If that happens, stick to your guns and remember why you turned down the offer in the first place.

THE LEGALITIES

If you change your mind, the company has the right to ask you to either work your notice (which is unlikely as you probably won't turn up) or they could start legal proceedings for breach of contract. While they may have a legal right to do this, I have never experienced or heard of a company actually doing it. Again, if a company does threaten you with legal action, you should seek professional advice.

RETRACTING THROUGH A RECRUITMENT CONSULTANT

If you got the job through a recruitment consultant, don't be afraid to be upfront about what's happening. As I've said previously, recruitment consultants hate it when they get 'radio silence' from a candidate. When that happens, they always know that something's wrong. Keep them fully informed if you are considering changing your mind. Of course. they will be disappointed and may try to talk you around, however, it will give them the opportunity to manage the relationship with their client, and you will maintain your professionalism.

You should always call them, not send email/text or worse, simply not turn up on the day you were due to start. That's totally unacceptable. Remember that consultants do blacklist candidates who aren't professional and share negative feedback with their counterparts in other recruitment companies. Not to mention the fact that not handling your withdrawal in a professional manner will undoubtedly damage your reputation with the employer. You never know when you may come across the same people again in future. It's a small world out there!

WHAT NEXT?

*"If it's important you'll find a way…
if not, you'll find an excuse."*

KEEPING UP MOMENTUM

It's easy to feel motivated in the first couple of weeks of a job search. Looking for the right job is front loaded as there are more activities at the beginning e.g. writing your CV, meeting recruitment consultants, joining websites, setting up your profile on LinkedIn and applying for numerous roles, etc. Once all those tasks have been completed, and job hunting turns into more of a maintenance function, it's fairly typical to hit a slump especially if you've received some rejections in the early days.

If this happens to you, it's worth revisiting the 'change curve' from Chapter 1 to remind yourself that negative feelings are completely natural. Reassure yourself that they won't last; it's just part of a process that you're going through; the most important thing is to keep going and not to get disheartened.

KEEPING MOTIVATED

1. **Stick to your plan** – Make sure that you complete a 'Daily Action Plan' at the beginning of the week and add to it as the week goes on. *'What gets written down gets done'* so having a plan that you stick to will help ensure that you don't waste time carrying out tasks that won't enhance your job search.

   I had one client who spent weeks perfecting his CV rather than starting his job hunt. That was because he was comfortable working on his CV, but the thought of job hunting was daunting. Therefore, until I intervened, he continued to do what he felt more at ease with.

2. **Plan your day** – If you're out of work, you should carry out your job search, at least two hours a day, Monday to Friday between 10.00 am to 12.00 noon. If you arrange a morning meeting, move your job hunt activities to the afternoon.

   If you're currently working, do your CV and register with on-line sites, created your LinkedIn profile, etc. at the weekend. Subsequently, you should work at least half an hour a day on your job hunt activities, either before or after work and make time during the day to call agencies/contacts by utilising your breaks effectively.

3. **Log your progress** – Remember to log your completed activities e.g. jobs you applied for, conversations with recruitment consultants and contacts, etc. Keep a copy of your record with you when you're out and about. That way, if you get a call regarding a job, you'll have the information to hand and will be able to speak to the caller with confidence.

4. **Update your CV on job sites** – Every week or, at least, every two weeks; you should upload your CV to job websites again. Many recruiters enter date parameters when searching for candidates, looking for the most recent people to join the site. Uploading a new CV a minimum of every two weeks will mean that you will always remain at the top of searches. Add this activity to your 'Daily Action Plan.'

5. **Always answer your phone** – During your job search always make it a priority to have your phone with you and answer it quickly and politely. I realise it's not always possible, therefore, if you have a voicemail facility, make sure that you turn it on and that your message is polite and professional. Ring the person back as soon as possible – try not to leave it until the next day, even if it's late, call them so that they know that you're motivated.

Often, where the caller is ringing from a landline, either 'No Caller ID' or 'Unknown' will show on your phone. If you don't usually answer these types of calls, I suggest that you make an exception during your job search.

6. **Don't stop applying** – Even if you think you've secured a role, don't stop your job hunting activities. Ending your search after receiving a verbal offer is a huge mistake and one that many people make. Never turn down an opportunity until you've received an employment contract and signed on the dotted line. Until that point, anything can happen.

7. **Keep in touch with your contacts** – Don't just ring them once and forget about them. Call them every few weeks and remember to tell as many people as possible (in a positive way) about your job search. People can't help if they don't know that you're looking.

8. **Take time out** – It's important that you take some time out to enjoy the time you have off if you aren't working. Before you know it you'll be back to work, wondering what you did with the time. Far from disrupting your job search, doing something that you enjoy will keep you focused and motivated. Exercise is particularly useful when you're feeling stressed or overwhelmed.

9. **Review your interview performance** – As soon as you can after

an interview, make a note of what went well and your development areas. Learn from the experience and incorporate that information into your next interview preparation (if necessary).

10. **Ask for feedback** – It's perfectly acceptable to ask for feedback after an interview. Recruiters will usually be quite candid about your performance, however, if they are reluctant to try asking, *"If there was one thing I could have done better, what would it have been?"* Again, incorporate any development areas into your preparation for your next interview.

11. **Don't beat yourself up –** If you've done everything you can to prepare for an interview and you still don't get the job, it just means that there was someone who had more experience or who was more qualified. Rather than beating yourself up, know that there's nothing else you could have done and be proud that you prepared so well. Don't let it knock your confidence; that job simply wasn't the right one for you.

12. **Be creative** – Try a mixture of all the job hunt activities I've mentioned and add any of your own. Feel free to contact me at info@whatnextconsultancy.co.uk if you think there's something that should be included in future versions of this book.

13. **Be patient** – Although we are starting to see glimpses that the recent recession is finally coming to an end, it's still a tough

market out there. Don't give up, stick to your plan and keep going; the right thing will come along.

14. **Visualise a positive outcome** – I know that I've mentioned it numerous times throughout the book, but visualisation is an essential tool. You should imagine your perfect outcome in as much detail as possible and run that mini video in your mind as many times as possible during the day.

    If you're going for an interview or presentation, again, visualise it going perfectly. *'The mind can't tell the difference between something real and something vividly imagine.'* Therefore, the more you practise through visualisation when you come to the real thing, your body is likely to go on autopilot, and you will deliver an excellent performance.

15. **Be positive –** Surround yourself with positive people and ignore the doom-mongers. *'We get what we think about'* therefore, it's important to stay optimistic to achieve a positive result. Being around positive people will boost your self-confidence and help you through potential difficult periods.

FREQUENTLY ASKED QUESTIONS

My colleagues and I get asked so many questions during our workshops and one-to-one sessions, many of which are repeated time and time again. Here is a selection of the most frequently asked questions:

Q: *I've worked for the same company for 20 years (although I've had various jobs in that time). Will a new employer see that as a negative?*

A: It really does depend on the recruiter; however, more importantly, it depends on how you position it. Some people may view it as a negative i.e. they may think that you only know one way of doing things or that you are set in your ways; however, it's up to you to demonstrate your versatility.

Research how things are done in other companies and review current industry/profession best practice. This is where networking helps; if you know someone who does your role or a similar one in another company, call them and meet them for coffee. Get as much information from them as possible around techniques and practices used in their business. If you have had various positions, make sure that you can demonstrate your skills through your achievements in your previous roles too (particularly if they were less than 3-5 years ago) so that the recruiter can see your adaptability.

Rather than seeing your longevity as a negative, many employers will view it as a positive as it indicates that you're loyal and are likely to stay with the company.

Q: *I've had lots of jobs in the same company, how do I explain that on my CV?*

A: Write the roles in the same way as you would if they were external. Review Chapter 3 to understand how much information you should include within your current and previous positions.

Q: *I've had lots of jobs in different companies, and I'm worried that employers will think that I have no staying power. What can I do about this?*

A: First of all, you need to decide what you really want to do and the type of company you want to work for. The 'Get Clear' exercise described in Chapter 2 is designed specifically for this. Once you're clear about the job you want, revise your CV, tailoring it to those types of roles. You may wish to consider not including every role you've ever had as it could make your CV look too busy. Remove older positions, especially if they have no bearing on what you are applying for now.

If asked why you've had so many jobs, a good way to answer is to say that you've tried different things to establish what you really want to do. Say that you've made a firm decision and are committed to finding and securing a job as an 'X.' However, be prepared to be able to explain the reasons for your decision.

Q: *I've had a career gap – I went travelling/took time off to look after my sick relative – how should I explain that on my CV?*

A: Be truthful and write it on your CV as a career gap. Companies see travelling as a bonus as it shows that you're adventurous, you can work on your own initiative, that you're outgoing and actively seek out new opportunities. As for looking after a relative, no ethical company will have a problem with that as it shows a strength of character, caring nature, and loyalty. If a company does have an issue with you taking a career break, you have to consider whether it's a company you want to work for. Is there a possible 'values' clash?

Q: I've recently taken time out of work to have and raise my child/children. How should I explain that on my CV?

A: I suggest that you write 'Career Break' and the dates. Remember that it's illegal for a company to discriminate against you for having children.

Q: *I've been out of work for a while, will that look bad to a prospective employer?*

A: Increasingly people are taking 'time out' after being made redundant. For most, it's the first time in their careers that have the opportunity to take a significant time off work legitimately. Many decide to go travelling, carry out work in the house, spend time with their family, and that's perfectly fine. Most employers won't have a problem with that, and if they do, again you have to ask yourself if that's the type of company for whom you wish to work. It's a more palatable way to explain periods of unemployment, rather than saying that you couldn't find a job.

Q: *I've been in interim roles for the last few years, and now I want a permanent job. Do you think I'll have a problem getting a permanent position?*

A: It's likely that a company will be concerned that you might not stay in a permanent position. You might have to convince them that you want to settle down and that theirs is the right job/company for you.

To do this, consider telling them that you've enjoyed your time gaining a wealth of experience that you wouldn't have been able to acquire in just one company. Inform them that you're now looking to settle down and utilise your skills and experience to make a difference in one company.

Q: *An agency has contacted me regarding a temp-to-perm (temporary to permanent) role, but I want a permanent position, should I still go for the interview?*

A: Absolutely! A temp to perm role is a relatively risk-free way to find out if you like the company and the position. It's a win/win scenario for both you and the company.

Q: *If I take a temporary/interim or contract role, will it affect my chances of a permanent role in the future?*

A: It shouldn't affect it. An employer will see that you haven't been out of work for long, and, therefore, your skills and experience are in demand. It also indicates that you have a strong work ethic which is appealing to a recruiter. It's also often easier to find a job when you're in one, as there won't be as much pressure on you to earn; therefore, you're likely to be more relaxed and come across as more confident in interviews.

Q: *If I take an interim/temporary or contract role, what should I do if a permanent role comes up that suits me better?*

A: If you a accept a non-permanent position, the employer will expect you to be committed and stay until the agreed end date. However, they are usually flexible on allowing you take time out for interviews towards the end of the contract (although it's unlikely that they will pay you for the time).

If you do secure a permanent role when you have a significant amount of time left on your current contract, you need to make a decision based on what's right for you in the long run, even if that means upsetting your current employer. Conduct yourself in a professional manner and bear in mind that you may need a reference from them too.

Q: *What's the difference between 'interim', 'fixed term' and 'temporary work'?*

A: They're all similar in that they are all temporary rather than permanent. Interim, however, tends to be on-going, without a fixed end date, unlike fixed term and both tend to attract a salary and benefits similar to those of the equivalent permanent role. Temporary work tends to be hourly paid and more flexible or ad hoc than the other two.

Q: *What's the difference between 'interim/fixed term' and 'contract' work?*

A: With an 'interim' role you will usually be offered the same pay and terms and conditions as the equivalent permanent position. If a company requires some general, non-management skills to support day to day activities, then they will usually employ an interim on a fixed term or ongoing basis.

'Contract' roles attract a daily rate of pay rather than a salary with benefits. Contracting often requires specific professional skills, usually to work on/complete a particular project or piece of work with a deadline.

When contracting it's likely that you'd need to set up a limited company or get paid through an umbrella company. Setting up your own limited company is relatively easy; however, you should speak to a good accountant about the legal requirements. Most will provide free advice up front, which can be invaluable.

I often recommend contract work to senior management/professional clients, as it can be lucrative and flexible. Contract/daily rate roles usually pay more than the equivalent permanent position, but you need to be mindful that you won't receive any benefits such as sick pay, holiday pay, pension *and* you have to pay your own taxes.

As employers will be paying a premium for your services, it's worth remembering that they tend to expect more from you than a regular employee. Therefore, it's important to set clear boundaries at the beginning regarding the hours you are prepared to work, how much travel you are willing to do and whether you are happy to stay away from home if required, etc.

You also need to be excellent at managing your money. **If you spend every penny you earn, then I do not advise contracting**. You have to keep a chunk of money back each month to fund the times you may be out of work. You also need to be able to pay your business expenses including:

- Corporation tax
- VAT (if you plan on earning more than £70,000 pa, then it's likely that your accountant will register your company for VAT)
- Personal tax return

Contract work can have its downsides, not least the fact that at the end of each contract, you're effectively out of work again. Therefore, to be able to keep in constant work, you need either a good network/excellent networking skills or have a profession that's in demand.

Q: *I know what you've said about keeping my CV to two pages, however, I've got lots of experience in numerous different areas, and I want the employer to know about it. Why can't I include it?*

A: Your CV is your primary marketing tool – the document that will hopefully get you an interview. Therefore, you should only contain information that backs up your skills and experience which corresponds to the role requirements. Everything else they'll see as 'noise', and it won't help you to secure an interview. Save your other great skills, achievements and experience to discuss at interview.

Q: *I'm sixty years old and just found out that my role is being made redundant. What can I do to increase my chances of getting a job?*

A: This is a common question – older job seekers frequently report feeling that they are on the 'scrap heap' and that 'no-one's going to want them.' That simply isn't true!

1. It's illegal to discriminate against someone because of their age. If you follow the instructions I've given in the CV writing section of this book, you won't have put every role you've ever had on your CV. Nor will you have put your date of birth or your education dates.

Therefore, at CV sifting stage a recruiter will have no idea how old you are. As long as you have the skills and experience they're looking for clearly outlined in your CV, there's no reason you shouldn't get selected for an interview.

2. There are no 'Jobs for Life' anymore. Companies are no longer looking for people to work for them for the next 20 years. Most employers know that if they manage to keep someone in the post for two/three years, they're doing well. Therefore, age is less relevant than it ever was.

3. Position yourself as an expert. You have lots of valuable life experience and skills, be very clear about what they are, and make sure that you've done your preparation thoroughly so that you get the information across in the right way.

4. Be positive and have confidence in your abilities. There's no bigger turn-off for a recruiter than someone who is negative and seems to have given up. If you think and feel like you're on the scrap heap, then that's how you will come across. You have a lot to offer, be clear about what that is, why they should give you the job and act like it!

5. Consider contract work if you're a professional, a middle/senior manager or have a particular set of desirable skills e.g. project management. It may be an ideal way to ease into retirement while earning good money. See *'What's the difference between 'interim' and 'contract' work?'* above for more information.

Q: I got dismissed by my previous company, what should I tell a prospective employer?

A: As there are so many factors and reasons why people are dismissed, it's difficult for me to give a 'catch all' answer to this question. Therefore, I would suggest that you speak to a professional career management coach or ACAS for advice on your particular circumstances.

ADDITIONAL RESOURCES

- 'Get Clear' Template
- Power Words
- CV Template
- Contact Spreadsheet - Networking
- Contact Spreadsheet – Recruitment Consultants/Agencies
- Job Application Tracker
- Daily Action Plan
- Covering Letter 1 – Speculative Applications
- Covering Letter 2 – Specific Applications
- Letter of Resignation

(N.B.: please remember to refer to the 'Notes' at the end of this section.)

GET CLEAR

Job Content (The 'tasks' you will be carrying out - day to day activities/responsibilities)			
What you want	*	**What you DON'T want**	*

The Company (Values, people, development, location, environment, etc.)			
What you want	*	**What you DON'T want**	*

Remuneration (Salary and benefits e.g. pension/holidays/shares/health care, etc.)			
What you want	*	**What you DON'T want**	*

POWER WORDS

Accelerated	Directed	Innovated	Recruited
Accomplished	Doubled	Installed	Redesigned
Administered	Earned	Introduced	Reduced
Analysed	Edited	Invented	Reorganised
Approved	Eliminated	Launched	Researched
Budgeted	Established	Led	Resolved
Built	Evaluated	Maintained	Revised
Completed	Excellent	Managed	Set-up
Conceived	Expanded	Modified	Simplified
Conducted	Facilitated	Motivated	Started
Consolidated	Financed	Negotiated	Streamlined
Controlled	Forecast	Operated	Strengthened
Converted	Formulated	Organised	Stretched
Convinced	Founded	Originated	Structured
Coordinated	Generated	Persuaded	Succeeded
Created	Headed	Planned	Summarised
Cut	Identified	Presented	Supervised
Delegated	Implemented	Processed	Trained
Delivered	Improved	Produced	Transformed
Demonstrated	Improvised	Programmed	Utilised
Designed	Increased	Promoted	
Developed	Influenced	Proposed	
Devised	Initiated	Purchased	

CV STRUCTURE – PAGE 1

[YOUR NAME]
[Address]
[Mobile] [Email]

SUMMARY STATEMENT

[This section should introduce you and your overall career journey. Remember to include a summary of your key strengths and relevant experience.] Top tip: What you are? What's different about you? What's next for you?

KEY SKILLS

- Skill 1
- Skill 2
- Skill 3
- Skill 4
- Skill 5
- Skill 6
- Skill 7
- Skill 8

CAREER SUMMARY

[This section should introduce you and your overall career journey. Remember to include a summary of your key strengths and relevant experience. Don't just list your duties ... your CV should be achievement focused]

[Job Title] **[Dates]**
[Company Name, Location[

[Details of Position – summarise 'what your job is' in one paragraph *Top Tip: What would you say you do if I met you outside work?*]

Achievements
- [Using bullet points, list up to eight of your most significant achievements in the role. Top Tip – What you did and what was the outcome]

[Job Title] **[Dates]**
[Company Name, Location[

[Details of Position – summarise what you did in a paragraph]

Achievements
- [See achievements above]

CV STRUCTURE – PAGE 2

[Job Title] **[Dates]**
[Company Name, Location[

[Details of Position – summarise 'what is your job' in a paragraph]

Achievements

- [See achievements above]

[Job Title] **[Dates]**
[Company Name, Location]

[Job Title] **[Dates]**
[Company Name, Location]

[Job Title] **[Dates]**
[Company Name, Location]

[Job Title] **[Dates]**
[Company Name, Location]

EDUCATION/PROFESSIONAL QUALIFICATIONS/TRAINING

Dates/Qualification

- [Details of education completed]

ADDITIONAL INFORMATION

- [Use this section to include interesting general information about yourself or your life achievements]
- [Include voluntary work, hobbies, and outside interests, particularly when you have won an award, taken part in some special event or done something out of the ordinary.]
- [Don't list: socialising, reading, cinema ... everyone does those!]
- [This section is optional - Don't include it if you've nothing interesting to say]

CONTACT SPREADSHEET – NETWORKING

Contact Spreadsheet

Name	Company	Phone number	Call 1 Date	Call 2 Date	Meeting Date	Follow Up Date	What We Discussed

CONTACT SPREADSHEET – CONSULTANTS/AGENCIES

Contact Spreadsheet - Recruitment Consultants/Agencies

Consultant	Agency	Phone number	Call 1 Date	Call 2 Date	Follow Up Date	Meeting Date	What We Discussed

JOB APPLICATION TRACKER

Job Applications

Date	Job Title	Company	Source (Paper/Agency/ Direct/Speculative/ Company/On-line)	Int'view Yes/No	1st Int'view Date	2nd Int'view Date	Notes

DAILY ACTION PLAN

Daily Action Plan

Date w/c		Action 1	Done	Action 2	Done	Action 3	Done	Action 4	Done	Action 5	Done
11-Jan	Monday	Call Jane	✓	Call Andy	✓	Call Lauren	✓	Call Reed Recruitment	✓	Apply for 4 jobs - Reed	✓
	Tuesday	Call Leanne	✓	Call Leyla	✓	Call Carley	✓	Call Hays Recruitment	✓	Apply for 4 jobs - Glass Door	✓
	Wednesday	Call Ben	✓	Call H2	✓	Call Reed	✓	Call Frazer John Recruitment	✓	Apply for 4 jobs - Totaljobs	
	Thursday										
	Friday										
18-Jan	Monday										

JOB APPLICATION COVERING LETTER

[Your Name]
[Your Address]
[Your Phone No] [Your Email]

[Date]

[Name]
[Company]
[Address]

Dear **[Name]**

Ref: [Job reference and job title]

Further to your advertisement in the [**name the source**], I would like to apply for the position of **[job title]** and attach my **[Curriculum Vitae/application form]** for your consideration.

As you will see from my CV, I am currently working for **[company]** as a **[current job title].** In my present position I am responsible for **[very brief summary relating back to the skills they require]**.

[Explain briefly, your greatest achievements which again relate to the job you are applying for]

With my proven ability to **[put your key skill(s) that relate to the job]**, I feel that I would be able to make a significant contribution to your company

Should you require any further information, please do not hesitate to contact me. In the meantime, I look forward to hearing from you.

Yours sincerely

[Your name]

SPECULATIVE APPLICATION COVERING LETTER

[Your Name]
[Your Address]
[Your Phone Number] [Your Email]

[Date]

[Name]
[Company]
[Address]

Dear **[Name]**

I wish to enquire whether you have a vacancy in your company for **a [your job title]**. I enclose a copy of my CV for your consideration.

As you will see from my CV, I am currently working for **[company]** as a [current job title]. In my present position I am responsible for **[very brief summary relating back to the skills they require]**.

[Explain briefly, your greatest achievements which again relate to the job you are applying for]

With my proven ability to **[put your key skill(s) that relate to the job]**, I feel that I would be able to make a significant contribution to your company

I would be grateful if you would contact me if you have any suitable vacancies. Alternatively, I would appreciate it if you could keep my information on file in case of future openings. I look forward to hearing from you.

Yours sincerely

[Your name]

RESIGNATION LETTER

[Your Name]
[Your Address]
[Your Phone Number]

[Date]

[Name]
[Company]
[Address]

Dear **[Name]**

I wish to tender my resignation as of today's date. As I understand it, my notice period is **[weeks/months]** and therefore, I intend my last working day to be **[date].**

I would like to take this opportunity to thank you and the company for your support and wish you well for the future.

Yours sincerely

[Your name]

Notes on Additional Resources:

- Where I have added brackets [ ] they should be removed from your final document – they are there to indicate where you need to add your information.
- Any sections of letters that I've highlighted in **bold** are to draw your attention to where you need to add your own content. You should remove the **bold** in your finished document other than to highlight your name at the end of letters.
- Where I've used **bold** in the CV template, you should keep it to highlight headings.

REFERENCE LINKS

Visit the book website and sign up with a quality email address for free access to a range of templates and information that work hand-in-hand with this book. They are specifically designed to help Land Your Dream Job:

www.yourdreamjob.co.uk

For more information on the services that What Next Consultancy provides (including one-to-one transformational and career coaching with Jo herself) and to read testimonials about how her coaching has helped her clients, visit:

www.whatnextconsultancy.co.uk

You can also sign up for the What Next Newsletter, a monthly email which includes hints and tips for leading a healthier, more productive and happier life. You can also keep up-to-date with Jo's most recent tips and advice by reading her blog at:

www.whatnextconsultancy.co.uk/blog

- **Website Design**:
  - Group Dane - www.groupdane.co.uk
- **Employment Law Advice**:
  - ACAS - www.acas.org.uk - Helpline 0300 123 1100
- **Right to Work documentation**:
  - www.gov.uk
- **Job Centre Plus:**
  - www.direct.gov.uk/en/Employment/Jobseekers/
- **Citizen's Advice Bureau:**
  - www.citizensadvice.org.uk/
- **Mind Mapping programme:**
  - www.xmind.net/
- **Kübler-Ross:**
  - www.ekrfoundation.org/
- **LinkedIn:**
  - www.linkedin.com

Recruitment Agencies/Consultancies and Online Job Sites:

- www.totaljobs.com
- www.reed.co.uk
- www.indeed.co.uk
- www.monster.co.uk
- www.kellyservices.co.uk
- www.jobsite.co.uk
- www.pertemps.co.uk

- www.glassdoor.co.uk
- www.michaelpage.co.uk
- www.hays.co.uk
- www.roberthalf.co.uk
- www.pertemps.co.uk
- www.forrest-recruitment.co.uk
- www.manpower.co.uk
- www.reed.co.uk
- www.bluearrow.co.uk
- www.adecco.co.uk

Video Conferencing

- www.skype.com
- www.bluejeans.com

ACKNOWLEDGMENTS

Firstly, I'd like to thank my fabulous long-time friend and colleague, Michelle Kirby. Not only has she contributed significantly to the content of this book, but she is always there to provide help and support (and copious amounts of Prosecco) when I'm most in need. I can't talk about Michelle without mentioning the rest of the gorgeous Kirby family, Mark, Emily and Laura. Love you guys.

Next, I must thank my wonderful web designer, business owner, author and friend, Dane Brookes. His help and advice continue to be invaluable, not to mention the design of the book cover and amazing, innovative websites that his company, Group Dane (www.groupdane.com) has created for me.

Thanks to my lovely ladies, Sharon Cunningham, Jo Cranham and Justine Williams for your continued love and support.

I'd like to express my gratitude to Debbie Hinbest, Lyndsay Chambers and Diane Hall for your continued faith and trust in my abilities. My business would not be where it is today without your support.

A big thank you to Michael Oliver, Vanessa Jackson, Noreen Spencer and Anna Kelly (recruitment consultants extraordinaire) for their input and invaluable examples of 'what not to do' as a candidate. Thanks also to my many clients past and present, who have unknowingly contributed to this book.

Finally, I'd like to thank my dad for his enduring love and support. I love you, dad.

ABOUT THE AUTHOR

Jo Banks, a Business Owner, Transformational Coach, NLP Master Practitioner, CBT Therapist and author has more than 20 years experience as a Senior HR Professional, establishing her own Coaching and Consultancy Practice, What Next Consultancy (UK) Ltd in 2009. With experience of working within a range of industries, Jo has a strong track record in positively creating high-performance cultures and dealing with complex people issues.

Jo is passionate about helping individuals and organisations to reach their full potential, through her proven and innovative coaching style. While she has trained in the traditional coaching methods, through coaching approximately 1500 people, Jo has found her own unique style focusing on behavioural change and fundamentally changing clients' thought patterns to achieve tangible results, super-charging their performance and elevating their career or business to the next level.

Jo runs inspirational leadership development stand-alone workshops, which include conflict management, communication skills, effective leadership, team development, advanced influencing and communication skills. She has also developed year-long Leadership Programmes which incorporate revolutionary workshops backing up the learning with one-to-one coaching. All Jo's work focuses predominantly on challenging thoughts and perceptions providing a unique blend of information and practical techniques that can put into practice immediately.

As well as providing coaching and leadership development, Jo has developed innovative Outplacement and Redeployment programmes which she and her colleagues deliver to organisations experiencing organisational change. She has combined her knowledge of recruitment (gained from interviewing thousands of people throughout her HR career), plus her insider knowledge of the recruitment industry, with her unique style of coaching to design unique programmes that deliver exceptional results.

'Land Your Dream Job Now!' is Jo's second book and describes the very best of her career management techniques. It provides easy to follow guidelines designed to enhance personal effectiveness putting readers streets ahead of their competitors, enabling them to *'Land Their Dream Job.'*

Jo's first book *'Thoughts Become Things: Change Your Thoughts Change Your World'* is also available at Amazon. It centres on the principles that she uses in her unique style of coaching. It is geared towards changing thoughts and behaviours by providing tools and techniques to understand better ourselves and others, to achieve exceptional results. A section of *'Thoughts Become Things'* is included at the back of this book, so keep reading!

Visit www.whatnextconsultancy.co.uk/testimonials to see for yourself the fantastic feedback Jo receives on a consistent basis.

CONNECT WITH JO

Twitter: @JoBanks247

LinkedIn: https://uk.linkedin.com/in/jo-banks-738b4412

Facebook: https://www.facebook.com/What-Next-150038221675653/?ref=hl

Web 1: www.yourdreamjob.co.uk

Web 2: www.whatnextconsultancy.co.uk

Web 3: www.thoughtsbecomethings.co.uk

Blog: www.whatnextconsultancy.co.uk/blog

'THOUGHTS BECOME THINGS'

An edited extract from Jo Banks' first book.

THOUGHTS BECOME THINGS

Change Your Thoughts... Change Your World

JO BANKS

CHAPTER 5

"The mind can't tell the difference between what's real and what's vividly imagined."

HOW TO CHANGE YOUR EMOTIONS QUICKLY

Do you ever wish that you didn't feel so tired, or that you could change how you're feeling or simply feel more positive?

As we've already discussed, there is a close link between what you do with your body and your emotions. In fact, your physiology (body language, facial expressions, breathing, etc.) and your emotions are so inextricably linked that if you want to immediately change your 'state' (how you're feeling), you can do it rapidly simply through changing your physiology.

Some of our physiology, such as walking, talking and how we hold our body is within our control and is driven by our conscious mind, and therefore, we can change it if we want to. Other behaviours are controlled entirely by our subconscious, for example, turning red when we feel embarrassed. In terms of our brain, our limbic system is where our base emotions and most of our automatic body language originates - it's the limbic system that's responsible for our fight or flight response. The fight or flight response is a physiological reaction that occurs in response to a perceived harmful event, attack, or threat to survival.

Often men and women who suffer extreme stress over prolonged periods (i.e. they are consistently triggering their flight/fight response) may experience reproductive issues as their body regularly diverts resources away from that area to other larger organs that need it. This process occurs in the limbic system and happens entirely unconsciously. People who receive a shock suddenly go pale again; this is because the subconscious is diverting blood away from the skin to other important organs in preparation for flight or flight. Suddenly going pale proves the interconnectedness between thoughts and physiology.

CHANGE YOUR 'STATE'

If I said, "Behind door A is someone who is depressed, describe how they look," you would probably say, "head low, shoulders slumped, shallow breathing, sad expression..." If I said, "Behind door B is someone who's really cheerful, describe how they look," you would say the opposite, "head up, eyes bright, happy expression" etc. Whatever emotions you experience, your body follows and vice versa. The great thing about having this information is that in any moment you can change how you feel by changing your physiology.

Shortly after I first came across this concept, I was driving home after a 12-hour day thinking how tired I was and then I remembered about changing my physiology to change my state. I looked at my body language and noticed I was slumped, my shoulders were down, and I was bent over, my blinking had slowed, and I was yawning every couple of minutes (yawning is our body's way of taking in more oxygen as our breath is more shallow when we're tired). I immediately adjusted my body, sat up straight, opened my eyes fully and took a few big deep breaths, smiled and instantly felt different. I was quite shocked at the difference just adjusting my body language and ***deciding*** not to be tired could make to improve my mood.

I use this technique constantly now, with both my clients and myself. It's especially useful to use with workshop delegates in the dreaded afternoon 'slump slot' just after lunch. I get them to do an exercise that involves moving their body - *motion creates emotion* - and they are then usually much more awake and receptive to learning more.

Since I learned this technique, whenever I find myself slipping into any old negative physiology patterns, I sit up straight, put my shoulders back, smile and take a deep breath. It's so simple but makes a huge difference.

CHANGE YOUR EMOTIONS BY CHANGING YOUR PHYSIOLOGY

For the next three days, keep an eye on how you're feeling. If you start to feel any negativity, observe what you're doing with your physiology (your body, face, how you're breathing, etc.) and change it. Put your shoulders back, sit/stand up straight, take a deep breath in and smile.

You'll be amazed at how quickly you move from negativity to positivity and the more you practise this, the better you will become. It interrupts your usual negative pattern and again, will create new neural pathways moving you towards a naturally positive state.

MOTION CREATES EMOTION

Changing your physiology by getting up and moving is a great way to change your emotions especially if you're stressed or anxious.

Putting some distance between you and the problem can be beneficial when experiencing strong negative emotions such as anger or frustration. When anger starts to rise, your body sends out a shot of adrenaline; that goes back to the 'flight or fight' response, which is what prepares us to either run away from a threat or fight it. These days, however, we can't run away from issues or fight, so we end up with significant amounts of adrenaline coursing through our veins with nowhere for it to go. Those unused chemicals contribute towards aggression, anxiety, stress and if not addressed over the long term, can lead to depression as well as physical illnesses.

Getting your body moving will create changes in your biochemistry, which will counterbalance the effects of the adrenaline, and other chemicals released into the bloodstream when we experience strong negative emotions.

MANAGING ANGER & OTHER NEGATIVE EMOTIONS

Start to tune into your body; often there will be early warning signs like the quickening of your heartbeat or tightness in your chest or sweating palms that alert you to the fact that you're about to experience negative emotions.

Learn to notice these signs and excuse yourself immediately even if that means that you look a bit odd doing so (it's better to do that than potentially experience other harmful consequences). So I would suggest you go to the washroom or take a walk, preferably outside where you can get some fresh air. Removing yourself from the situation and the simple act of moving your body will help diffuse those negative emotions. It also acts as a pattern interrupt, as we discussed previously, if you keep interrupting your old patterns of behaviour, you'll develop new ones, and it will become harder to access the old ones.

If you can't physically remove yourself from a situation, try *visualising* going for a walk. To illustrate this, a client was explaining to me that she couldn't just get up and take a walk when she was feeling stressed or frustrated in an important meeting. However, she recognised the need to take a step back and disassociate herself from what was going on, at least for a short time. Therefore, she developed a method of *visualising* going for a walk that works for her.

She explained that she literally 'shuts down' in her mind for as long as it takes for her to mentally get up out of her seat, walk to the door, open it, walk to the stairs, walk down the stairs, out of reception. She'll then visualise walking around the block once (twice if she is feeling particularly stressed) coming back into the building, back up the stairs and back in the room, ready to re-join the discussion.

She says that no one knows what she is doing; they assume that she has zoned out for a while and is taking 'thinking' time. When she has done this little 'visualisation walk', she says that she has usually calmed down and is ready to join the discussion again with a more balanced viewpoint.

TAKE A HIKE & CHANGE YOUR BIOCHEMISTRY

Regular exercise is an amazing way to help you gain a more balanced perspective on any situation and to help you manage your emotions, as it helps burn off those unwanted chemicals produced by the flight or fight response. That's why doctors prescribe exercise for sufferers of depression; because it changes your biochemistry.

Cortisol is a hormone generated by the body under stress, such as anger, anxiety or fear and over a prolonged period it ultimately inflames and damages your organs. Exercise burns cortisol and adrenalin, leaving us healthier and happier. Exercise also stimulates the brain's pituitary gland to release endorphins into the bloodstream, calming us down and making us feel good. Endorphins are morphine-like hormone molecules that enter the brain's neurons and park on receptors that normally send pain–killing molecules back to other parts of the brain. It is thought that endorphins are even more powerful and yield a euphoric feeling than opiate drugs such as morphine and opium, which park on the same receptors when introduced to the body.

Exercise doesn't have to mean running a marathon or doing an hour's worth of hard labour in the gym; it can be anything that you do for around 10-20 minutes that increases your heart rate. That's why a walk around the block can be sufficient to make a real difference in the way you're feeling - see Chapter 5 for more on the power of exercise.

WHY WE SOMETIMES GO 'BLANK'

Are you one of those people who sometimes can't think quickly enough when someone says something that shocks or upsets you, and afterwards you think, "Why didn't I say X, Y, Z"? It's a typical response and something that I experience from time to time so I can appreciate how frustrating it is.

What's happening is that when the subconscious receives distressing information, it freezes for a moment while it processes it. A second or so later, your conscious brain will kick in, and you'll be able to respond, but it's often too late, and you've missed an opportunity to say what you really think.

If you know, this happens to you, the next time you 'freeze,' instead of trying to answer a question or give a coherent reply, tell the person that you need to think about what they have said and will get back to them. I tend to say, "I hear what you've said, I just need to process it. Can I come back to you?" That buys me some time to think of an appropriate response. It's a common problem and often knowing that there is a reasonable explanation for it helps us understand and deal with it in a more efficient way.

THE POWER OF VISUALISATION

I can't stress enough the power that visualisation has on our lives as *the mind can't tell the difference between something that's vividly imagined and something that's real.* Therefore, the more you practise visualising the outcome you want, the more likely you are to achieve it. The great thing about it is that it's easy to do, you can do it anywhere, and no-one needs to know you're doing it.

Visualising something creates new neural pathways in the brain as we discussed in Chapter 3. When you do something for the first time, whether you do it for real, or you visualise doing it, you create a new neural pathway. The more times you practise doing that thing, imagining it clearly in your mind, the deeper the neural pathway will become and the easier it will be to do in real life.

There has been so much research into the power of visualisation; you only need to look online, and you'll find pages and pages of evidence. Neuroscientists at Harvard carried out a piece of research where they taught a simple five-fingered combination of piano notes to a group of people, which they physically played over and over again for two hours a day for five consecutive days. Another group of volunteers didn't play the notes but imagined playing the same combination for the same practise time each day.

The researchers examined the brains of the volunteers every day using a technique known as TMS (Transcranial Magnetic Stimulation) and found that there was little or no difference between the brains of those who actually played the notes and those who visualised playing them. The brain areas in both cases grew significantly in size.

VISUALISE THE OUTCOME YOU DESIRE

You can use the same visualisation technique for any important event where you may be nervous or if you have to produce an outstanding performance. If a client has an important meeting, presentation or interview, etc., I always tell them to visualise the whole day going perfectly from beginning to end. Imagine your entire day in as much detail as possible from getting up, to getting dressed, to getting to the venue and setting up, giving your presentation/interview, etc. and everything else that you're planning to do that day.

Don't forget that it's important to visualise *everything going perfectly* - if you visualise anything negative, then that's what you're likely to experience when you come to the real thing. The more you visualise things going perfectly, by the time you come to the real thing, your mind already knows what to expect and exactly what you need to do because you've programmed it into your subconscious i.e. you've built a deep neural pathway.

If you feel nervous, which is natural, do the deep breathing exercise explained later in this chapter. Calm yourself down and let your subconscious take over - it's almost like switching to autopilot if you've practised visualising everything going well enough beforehand.

VISUALISATION & WORRY

If you're a worrier, I guess that you picture all the worst-case scenarios in microscopic detail. What you're doing when you're visualising all the catastrophes that *may* happen to you, is training your brain to react in a negative way, and you're creating deep neural pathways that make it easy to go into that 'victim' state, which attracts negative outcomes.

A client of mine had to give a speech at her daughter's wedding, and she was terrified - in fact, she was so upset that she cried while she was telling me about it and found it difficult to get her words out. I asked her what she was seeing (visualising) and what she was saying to herself when she thought about giving the speech. She said, *"I've been trying to think about all the things that could go wrong so that if they do go wrong on the day, I'll be prepared"*. I was horrified, what she was doing was programming herself for it to go wrong and having all the negative feelings and behaviours that went with it!

Because (again) *the mind can't tell the difference between what's real and what's vividly imagined* she was fully associated with it all going horribly wrong, and so she was upsetting herself to the point that she could barely speak. I told her she had to reverse her thinking and visualise everything going perfectly.

I got her to relax and imagine how the day would go if everything were perfect. I asked her to see, feel and hear everything going well in as much detail as possible creating a mini video in her mind. We did this a few times until she could access the 'video' clearly and instantly. I then told her to practise running that video as many times as she could before the wedding and to practise some simple confidence techniques that I had taught her.

She texted me on the evening of the wedding and told me that she had been completely in control of her emotions (although she did have a little cry in the church, that was an appropriate response, and so she was happy) and the speech went perfectly. Since then I'm glad to say that as a result of that short one-hour session with me, not only did her speech go well, but she is now able to stand up and present in front of people comfortably, something she has never been able to do before. Consequently, she has been able to expand her business by delivering profitable training sessions to other businesses, something that she would never have been able to do previously because of her irrational fear of public speaking.

Not only does visualising something going well repeatedly and significantly increase your chances of success, doing something over and over in your mind will also help you to spot and overcome any obstacles, allowing you the opportunity to change things before they become a problem. It is the difference between success and failure – it unlocks hidden potential.

The following exercise is a simple way to demonstrate the power of visualisation:

THE POWER OF VISUALISATION

Read this exercise through at least once before trying it so that you understand what you need to do:

1. Stand up straight with your feet, hips, torso, and head all facing the front.

2. Take your right arm and point forward at right angles to your body.

3. Twist your body around so that you're pointing as far as you

can reach behind you.

4. Make a mental note how far you've managed to point.

5. Return and put your arm down.

6. Close your eyes (sit down while you do this if you find you're a little unsteady standing up with your eyes closed) and imagine pointing much further - visualise clearly in your mind the new position that you want to point to.

7. Open your eyes and repeat numbers 1-5 and note where you are now able to point to.

Did you point much further after the visualisation? I'm sure you did. If this simple exercise demonstrates how much further you can point as a result of visualising the outcome you want (albeit merely pointing), imagine how much more you can achieve in your life if you adopt the habit of imagining achieving what you want on a consistent basis.

If you ask any successful person, they will tell you they imagined creating their multi-million selling widget or they have visualised running a multi-national corporation or "always dreamed" of owning their own business. Everything starts with a thought and envisioning how you want your life to be whether you're consciously aware of it or not. ***THOUGHTS BECOME THINGS!***

RELAXATION TECHNIQUES

Learning simple relaxation techniques is important to controlling your emotions and to dealing with and releasing stress, anxiety and tension. I've listed a few techniques that are simple to do and give immediate results. Obviously, the more you practise them, the easier they become and the quicker you'll find yourself in control of your emotions and in a relaxed state.

PROGRESSIVE MUSCLE RELAXATION

Progressive muscle relaxation is a technique that helps to release tension in the muscles bringing about deep feelings of relaxation. It's best done either sitting or lying down in a quiet place, preferably where you won't be disturbed. Wearing loose, comfortable clothing would also be beneficial. It's a great technique to do if you have trouble getting to sleep. Therefore, getting into the habit of doing it in bed, as part of your bedtime routine, is perfect.

FULL MUSCLE RELAXATION METHOD

Please read this whole exercise at least twice before you try it. The technique involves grouping the body into muscle groups i.e. legs, midsection, arms and head and systematically tensing and releasing each muscle in its muscle group, only moving on to the next muscle group once the current one feels totally relaxed. If you do this exercise fully, it should take around 20 minutes (if you haven't already fallen asleep part way through!).

You will tense each muscle twice, once for five seconds and then relax for 15 seconds and then tense that muscle again for a further five seconds, release again for 15 seconds and then move on to the next muscle. As you tense your muscles, pay close attention to any sensations that you may be experiencing in the muscles as they contract.

1. Starting with the feet and legs: tense and relax first your toes, then feet, then calf muscles, inner thighs, thighs and buttocks using the pattern mentioned above - then tense and relax the muscle group as a whole.

2. Moving to your arms: tense and relax your fingers, then your hands, biceps, triceps and your full arm - then tense and relax the muscle group as a whole.

3. Moving to your midsection: tense and relax your pelvic floor muscles, then your stomach and then your chest - then tense and relax the muscle group as a whole

4. Moving to your back: tense your lower back and then your

upper back - then tense and relax the muscle group as a whole.

5. Moving to your head: tense and release your neck, then your facial muscles, the top of your head - then tense and relax the muscle group as a whole.

Once all the muscles in each section have been tensed and released twice you should experience a feeling of deep relaxation.

BUY NOW FROM AMAZON

'Thoughts Become Things: Change Your Thoughts Change Your World' is available now, worldwide from Amazon in both Kindle and paperback versions. For more information visit:

www.thoughtsbecomethings.co.uk

Made in the USA
Charleston, SC
28 April 2016